Harcourt SOCIAL STUDIES Studies

Social Studies in Action

Resources for the Classroom

Grade 3

Harcourt

SCHOOL PUBLISHERS

www.harcourtschool.com

Printed in the United States of America

ISBN-13: 978-0-15-349420-8
ISBN-10: 0-15-349420-4

10 0982 16 15 14 13 12 11 10

Contents

Introduction

This *Social Studies in Action: Resources for the Classroom* booklet provides a variety of activities designed to help enhance students' understanding of events and issues throughout history. Some activities require students to take part in a historical event, while others allow students to write creatively on important social issues. Planning options are available in the back of the booklet. The following kinds of activities are included.

Bag Ladies Activity   These classroom activities are mini-workshops. Using simple household items, students review each unit by creating fun works of art.

Drama Activity   The classroom becomes a theater for this variety of reading activities. Drama activities include original plays written about scenarios in history and various adaptations.

Simulations and Games   Games allow students to review important material in a fun yet challenging way. Simulations place students directly in a historical situation and ask them to take sides, make decisions, and resolve conflicts.

Long-Term Project   The main idea of each unit is the focus of these four-week-long projects designed to integrate social studies in art.

Short-Term Projects   These projects are short and simple activities. Students explore different aspects of a unit through activities such as singing songs, drawing pictures, and making models.

Writing Projects   The main purpose of these projects is to provide writing practice. Unit content is used to facilitate various types of writing, from short stories to newspaper articles.

Daily Geography   This section provides a daily review of important concepts in geography.

Why Character Counts   These activities focus on a different character trait for each unit. Students read about and define each trait and complete an activity to reinforce understanding.

Economic Literacy   Students learn about important economic concepts related to each unit and complete an activity on sound economic principles.

Citizenship   This feature is divided into three sections. Students learn citizenship skills by reading, participating in a debate, and completing writing activities.

People and Places Pamphlet
Unit 1

Materials needed:

*Blank paper

*Crayons, markers, or colored pencils

*Scissors

*Glue

Social Studies Skills:

*Community People

*Location

*Community Story

Reading Skills:

*Summarize

*Sequence

*Main Idea and Details

Instructions:

1. Fold the blank sheet of paper into thirds.

2. Create a title page (cover) for the pamphlet.

Illustrations:

3. Students illustrate and write about people in their community and their jobs.

4. Students make a map of their community and may add important buildings and landmarks.

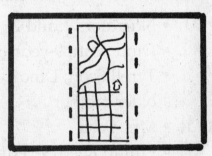

5. Students add the history of their community, telling how it was founded and by whom.

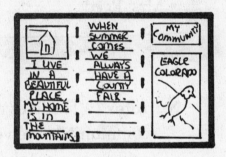

Good Morning!

A readers theatre play about three families who live in different areas of the country

Cast of Characters

- Narrators 1 and 2
- Dina Scott, 9-year-old girl
- Tyrell Scott, Dina's older brother
- Mrs. Scott
- Phillip Reed, 9-year-old boy
- Mrs. Reed

- Mr. Reed
- Brody Wicks, 9-year-old boy
- Mimi Wicks, Brody's younger sister
- Mr. Wicks
- Sound Effects

Narrator 1: The lives of people who live in different communities are very different. The Scott family lives on a farm in a rural community. The Reed family lives in the suburbs, and the Wicks family lives in an urban community.

Narrator 2: Let's join the Scott family for a normal morning on their farm.

Sound Effects: (sound of roosters crowing)

Dina: Time to get up, Tyrell. We have to do our chores.

Tyrell: (groaning) I just want to sleep. I don't want to go out and work today. If you do my chores today, I will do yours tomorrow.

Dina: Deal.

Tyrell: Great! Now let me go back to sleep.

Narrator 1: Dina walks out to the barn. When she gets there, she finds that her mom is already milking the cows.

© Harcourt

Dina: Good morning, Mom.

Mrs. Scott: Good morning, Dina. I need you to start feeding the chickens, while I finish milking the cows. Then we have to give the horses some fresh hay. I was going to have Tyrell start doing that. Where is your brother, by the way?

Dina: He's sleeping. I'm filling in for him today, and tomorrow he's going to take my place.

Mrs. Scott: Well, as long as the two of you have worked it out. I don't want any arguing tomorrow. Let's hurry. We have to finish these chores before the bus comes to pick you up for school.

Sound Effects: (sound of a yawn)

Mrs. Scott: I know you're tired because you have to get up so early every day, but I really am thankful for your help. Your dad and I couldn't run this farm without you and your brother.

Dina: It's a lot of work, but I wouldn't want to live anywhere else!

Narrator 2: Mrs. Scott smiles. She and Dina continue the morning chores in the barn. Then Dina goes back to the house to get ready for school.

Narrator 1: We've just seen what a morning with the Scott family is like. Now let's visit the Reed family to see what a morning in the suburbs is like.

Sound Effects: (sounds of a car driving down the street and birds chirping)

Phillip: Good morning, Mom. I'm so excited!

Mrs. Reed: Why is that?

Phillip: Remember, we are going on a field trip today to the science museum. Since our school is not far from the city, we get to go into the city to see the new dinosaur exhibit.

Mrs. Reed: I did remember your trip. I'm glad you're excited! It seems as if you are finally getting used to that new school of yours.

Phillip: Yes, I am. When we first moved to the suburbs, I didn't like it. But it's actually pretty cool here. I have made good friends in our neighborhood, and we live near my school.

Mr. Reed: What do you want to see at the museum today?

Phillip: I want to see the huge skeletons and displays of the dinosaurs. Our teacher said that the skeletons are bigger than we could ever imagine.

Mr. Reed: That sounds like fun. Do you have everything you need?

Phillip: Yes. I have my permission slip, and my lunch is packed. I think that's everything. Dad, can I go next door to Jason's house to wait for the bus?

Mr. Reed: I think that would be okay.

Phillip: See you later, guys!

Narrator 1: Phillip runs out of his house and over to Jason's house. He waits there for the school bus to come.

Narrator 2: We've seen two families. Now let's visit one more. The Wicks family lives in an urban area. Let's find out how they spend their morning.

Sound Effects: (sounds of car horns being honked)

Brody: Mimi, hurry up and eat your breakfast. I want to get to school on time, and you know you don't like to walk fast. We have to leave soon, so I can get there to set up my science project.

Mimi: I'm eating as fast as I can. I'm almost finished.

Mr. Wicks: Brody, let her finish her meal. I promise we won't be late.

Narrator 2: Mimi finishes eating. Then Brody, Mimi, and Mr. Wicks set off on their walk to school. They walk down five flights of stairs to get to the bottom floor of their apartment building. When they leave the building, they are standing on a crowded city street. People are walking by quickly, and drivers are honking their car horns.

Mr. Wicks: Brody, make sure you hold your sister's hand. I want to carry your project so it doesn't get ruined.

Brody: Thanks, Dad. Come on, Mimi. Keep up with me.

Narrator 1: Brody takes Mimi's hand, and the two walk with their father along the crowded street. People surround them everywhere. They pass a subway entrance and many shops, businesses, and apartment buildings. Finally, they arrive at school.

Mr. Wicks: Here we are, guys. I know you don't like to walk to school. If we lived somewhere else, you could ride a bus to school.

Brody: It's all right, Dad. I really do like the city. I wouldn't want to live anywhere else!

Narrator 2: Now you've seen three families who live in different communities. Think about the three families. How are their communities alike? How are they different? Which family lives in a community that is like your own?

The End

Simulations and Games

Town Meeting In this simulation, students assume the roles of people taking part in a public meeting on community issues. The topic of this meeting is how best to use a parcel of land that has recently become available in the community. Use realistic factors that pertain to your community to describe this parcel. Here are some questions to consider:

- Where is the land?
- How large is it?
- What is located nearby?
- What condition is the land in now?
- What are some needs of your community that might be met by this land?

Help students determine roles, such as mayor (who presides over the meeting); town council members (who may ask questions of presenters), and groups of citizens who favor different uses for the land (such as a playground, dog run, community garden, restaurant, shopping area, new housing, or museum). Give groups time to prepare what they will say and how they will get support for their ideas. Guide students by establishing ground rules for respectful give-and-take. Help them express their ideas, ask and field questions, and weigh the various choices to make a well-considered decision. **SIMULATION**

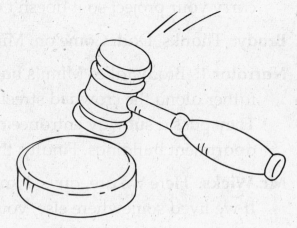

Guess My Community Divide the class into groups of four or five people. Designate one person in each group to be the mystery person. Have the mystery person choose one of the three types of communities discussed in the unit—rural, suburban, or urban. Tell the mystery person not to reveal his or her choice to the rest of the group members. Then, one at a time, have the other group members ask yes-or-no questions to help them figure out the mystery person's "secret location." After all the group members have had a turn to ask a question, have them try to guess the mystery person's location. Play should continue until everyone in the group has had a chance to be the mystery person. **GAME**

© Harcourt

Checker Directions

This game for two to four players reinforces directionality. Players need a basic checkerboard, checkers or other playing pieces, self-stick notes, and a spinner. Prepare a spinner with eight sections: two each for north, south, east, and west. Label each side of the checkerboard with the four basic directions. Use a self-stick note to highlight a square on the board (any) as the destination. (Change for each game.) Players randomly place their pieces anywhere on the board, at least four squares from the destination. The object of the game is to be the first player whose piece reaches the destination. Moves are determined by the spinner. For example, if the spinner says "north," the player moves the piece one square north of wherever it last was. Pieces may not jump or capture. They may not share a square. So if a move would require a player to land on a square already occupied, the player forfeits that turn. **GAME**

Mystery Map

This two-person game is a variation of "Battleship," played using the squares of a grid map rather than the points of a coordinate grid. Prepare reusable maps with a letter-and-number grid system. You can laminate real maps or superimpose grids on images. Each player secretly chooses a box on the map with a location that can be given as a letter and number, such as C-3 or A-4. Opponents take turns guessing the location of the secret box. By luck and through process of elimination, one player will eventually locate the secret box. As a variation, the whole class can play this game using an overhead projector. **GAME**

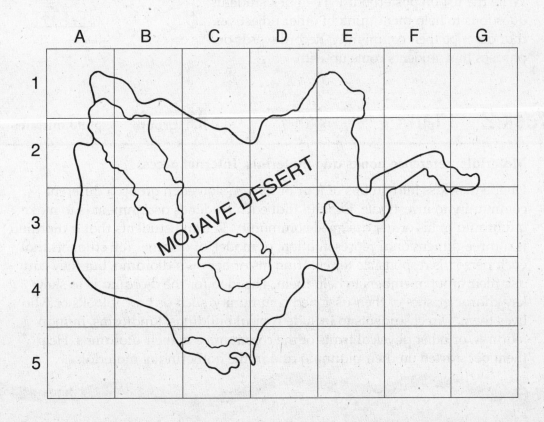

CLASS WALL: COMMUNITIES ALL AROUND US

Use this project to help students think in greater depth about the characteristics that define their own communities as well as the communities that surround them.

Week 1   Introduce
 class   30 minutes

Materials: posterboard, markers

Introduce the project by explaining that the class will be investigating many different types of communities during the next few weeks. Begin by brainstorming with students a list of characteristics that describe their community. Write the list on posterboard. Then ask students questions to help them think of other adjectives that describe their community. Record words or phrases that students come up with.

Week 2   Plan
 group   90 minutes

Materials: reference books and materials, Internet access

Divide the class into groups of four or five. Assign each group a different community to investigate. Explain that each student's assignment is to make a diorama of his or her assigned community. Remind students that a diorama is a three-dimensional representation, or model, of a scene. Tell students that each person is responsible for creating his or her own diorama, but they can ask their group members to help them. The idea for the diorama is to show key characteristics of their assigned community, such as how it looks or who lives there. Direct students to include typical buildings, landforms, human features, or other physical traits of the community in their dioramas. Help them get started on their planning and in the gathering of materials.

© Harcourt

Week 3   Finish Dioramas group 90 minutes

Materials: shoe boxes, paper, posterboard, pens, pencils, markers or colored pencils, craft sticks, glue, tape, any other needed art materials, reference books and materials, Internet access

Provide time for students to complete their dioramas. Allow them to search reference books for pictures of their communities to use as models. Assist students with creating their dioramas as needed. When students have completed their dioramas, ask them to prepare a list of words that describe the community they will present. Help students use reference materials to gather details and ideas. Have them present their list of words in the form of a poster.

Week 4   Present the Dioramas  class 90 minutes

Materials: posterboard, markers, camera (optional)

Before the presentation, have students make invitations for parents, caregivers, and other classes to view their displays. Help students display their dioramas and accompanying posters around the classroom. Give each student five minutes to talk about his or her diorama. Ask students to explain why they included the images they did and to tell what words they used to describe their community. Encourage students to ask questions of one another and to comment on their displays. After everyone has presented, have students stack their dioramas to form a wall. Explain that the wall represents the communities that surround them. If possible, conclude by taking photographs to make a bulletin board display or scrapbook of the project.

Tips for Combination Classrooms

 For Grade 2 students: Help students make an audio presentation with comments about how they made their dioramas.

 For Grade 4 students: Ask students to extend the project by making a diorama that represents a region of the United States. Have students make a list of words that describe their new diorama.

UNIT 1 Short-Term Projects

Use these projects to help students explore the different ways that places can be described.

Map It!

 individual  20 minutes

Materials: large construction paper, pens, pencils, markers, a map for reference

What is your community like? Have students make a map that shows their community. Guide them to think first about the places they need to include in a map of their community. Point out features that are usually included on maps, such as a key and a compass rose. Encourage students to create symbols to represent certain places in the community. Have students share their maps when they are complete.

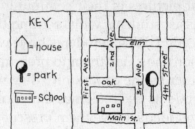

Regional Sort

 groups 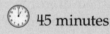 45 minutes

Materials: old magazines, catalogs, travel brochures, scissors, index cards or construction paper pieces, glue or paste

Discuss with students the similarities and differences among the terms *urban*, *suburban*, and *rural*. Then have them create sorting cards with images of urban, suburban, and rural scenes, or things typically associated with each area. For example, a picture of a tractor could represent *rural*; a high-rise apartment house would represent *urban*. Have students cut out the images and glue them to cards. Shuffle the cards, and ask other groups to sort them. Conclude by discussing the key features of each kind of region.

© Harcourt

My Dream Community

 individual   30 minutes

Materials: paper or index cards, markers or crayons, old magazines, scissors, glue or paste, hole punch, string, coat hanger

Remind students that people usually choose to live in a certain place because that place has characteristics that suit them. For instance, someone who loves to farm would probably choose to live in a rural community. Tell students to imagine they could live in any community in the world. Ask students to think about the type of place they would choose. Invite students to create mobiles that show the characteristics their dream community would have. Have students draw pictures or find pictures in old magazines. Then have students attach their pictures to index cards or sheets of paper. When students have finished drawing and finding pictures, assist them in hanging the pictures from the hanger to create the mobile.

Where Have We Been?

class   30 minutes

Materials: wall map of the United States, pushpins, chart paper, markers

Inform families that you plan to gather data about the different states of the United States where students in your class have ever lived or visited. This will help focus students on the task and enable them to get input from family members. Post a large map of the United States on a bulletin board. Provide pushpins. Invite students to add a pin to any state they have ever lived in or visited. Then count the pins in each state. List the data on chart paper, state by state. Then make a graphic organizer that shows how many different states children have been to. Discuss the data by posing questions such as: *Which is the farthest state anyone has been to? Which states has no one visited?* Vary the project by focusing on counties or cities in your state or on national parks, beaches, canyons, deserts, state capitals, and so on.

Writing Projects

Use these prompts to get students writing about communities.

Faraway Friends

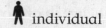 individual 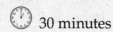 30 minutes

Explain to students that a pen pal is a friend who is made and kept through letters or e-mail. Tell students that a pen pal is usually someone who lives in another state or country. Have students imagine that they have a pen pal who lives in another country. Invite students to write letters to their pen pals describing their community. Tell students to be as descriptive as possible because their pen pals know very little about their community. Encourage students to ask questions about their pen pals' countries and communities. If possible, set up an actual pen pal program in your classroom in which students are able to correspond with students their age who live in another part of the country or world.

What Is a Community?

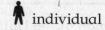 individual 30 minutes

Remind students that they have been learning about communities. Explain to students that a community is not just a place but is also the people who live in that place. Have students write an essay that answers the following two questions: What is a community? What does my community mean to me? Remind students that a good essay includes many details that help the author express ideas. Encourage students to use a graphic organizer to help them organize their thoughts before they begin writing.

Travel Pamphlet

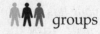 groups 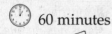 60 minutes

Collect and display some travel pamphlets to destinations of interest to your students. Then invite students to pick a destination and create their own travel pamphlet about it. Encourage them to include facts and details about the place, as well as activity ideas for visitors to the area. Pamphlets can include photographs or illustrations.

© Harcourt

Observation Journal

 class   🕐 60 minutes

Take the class outside on a nice day, and have students take along a notebook and a pencil. Go on a walk with the students near and around the school. Allow 15 minutes, during which students closely observe everything they see along the walk. Encourage them to notice sights, sounds, smells, and textures. While observing, students can jot down words or phrases or write complete sentences. Then, back in the classroom, have students use their observation notes to write a personal journal entry about everything they noticed. Ask students to describe how they felt at certain points along the walk as well as the things they saw.

Letter to the Editor

🧍 individual   🕐 45 minutes

Tell students that most newspapers invite readers to send in letters that discuss issues of concern to them. These letters are called "letters to the editor." Some of these letters are printed in the newspaper so that other readers can know how their neighbors feel about certain issues. Help students think of an issue about the neighborhood, town, or state that concerns them. It might be something like the need for safe bicycle paths or better street lamps in dark neighborhoods. Ask students to write a persuasive letter to the editor that expresses their concerns and offers ideas for improvements.

Picturing Stories

🧍 individual   🕐 30 minutes

Remind students that the communities in which people live often determine the activities people take part in and the jobs they do. Show students a picture of a community. Select a picture that clearly shows one type of community— rural, suburban, or urban. Ask students to think about the kinds of lives the people in the community lead. Have students write a story about the community shown in the picture. Encourage students to be as descriptive as possible in their writing.

Daily Geography

1. Location	What city is the capital of the United States?
2. Place	The people who live in the same community may have different cultures. What is a culture?
3. Place	What is a climate?
4. Place	What is a land that gets little rain called?
5. Place	What is a landform?
6. Location	Which two oceans are located near the East and West Coasts of the United States?
7. Human-Environment Interactions	Which landform is best described as a flat land: a mountain, a canyon, or a plain?
8. Place	Which is the largest body of water: a stream, an ocean, or a river?
9. Place	The United States is a nation made up of many communities. What is a nation?
10. Place	St. Louis, Missouri, and Bogor, Indonesia, are sister cities. What are sister cities?
11. Place	In 2004, a tsunami caused damage to many communities in Indonesia. What is a tsunami?
12. Location	What can you use a map to find out?
13. Location	What part of a map tells you direction?
14. Location	What are the four cardinal directions?
15. Location	What are the four intermediate directions?

© Harcourt

16. Regions   Communities are often located in different regions of the country. What is a region?

17. Human-Environment Interactions   What is a population?

18. Regions   Which is an urban area: a farm, a small town, or a city?

19. Movement   Which of these would be the most likely form of transportation for a person who lives in a rural area: a subway, a train, or a car?

20. Place   Along what river is the city of Baltimore located?

21. Human-Environment Interactions   San Francisco is a city on a bay. What is a bay?

22. Movement   What is transportation?

23. Movement   In which direction would you travel if you went in a straight line from Michigan to Alabama?

24. Location   Which states border North Carolina?

25. Place   What does a grid map show?

26. Place   What is a suburb?

27. Location   Maplewood is a town in New Jersey. It is located very close to New York City. Which type of community is Maplewood: urban, suburban, or rural?

28. Place   What is a rural community?

29. Location   In which state is the city of Little Rock?

30. Human-Environment Interactions   What is agriculture?

© Harcourt

Why Character Counts

Caring

Communities should be caring places. It's not only the very old, the very young, or the very sick who need people to help them. Lots of people need help in lots of ways. Caring for others is a job we all should do gladly and freely. Caring for those in need can bring out the best in us.

Some cities in the United States have sister cities in other countries. St. Louis, Missouri, and Bogor, Indonesia, are sister cities. They share ideas and work together to help others in need. When a tsunami caused damage in Indonesia, St. Louis was eager to help. The people of St. Louis showed support by sending money and supplies to those in need.

- **Trustworthiness**
- **Respect**
- **Responsibility**
- **Fairness**
- ✓**Caring**
- **Patriotism**

In Your Own Words:

Have you helped someone in need? Have you cared for a sick or hurt animal? Have you given your time to help a good cause? Write about an experience you have had as a caring citizen.

_____

_____

_____

© Harcourt

Name _____

∽— Character Activity ∽

Answer the following questions. Write your answers on the blank lines.

1. What different kinds of places in your community offer care to others?

_____

_____

_____

_____

2. What are some of the services these places provide?

_____

_____

_____

3. What are some ways for children your age to help others? Describe them.

_____

_____

_____

_____

Economic Literacy

Location and Choice

Some families like to live in the city. Other families like to live in the country. Some families choose to live in the suburbs. Every location has something to offer. Families must decide which place fits what they want.

The Chen family has six people. There are two parents, a grandmother, and three children. Mr. Chen is a barber. Mrs. Chen is an art teacher. Grandmother is retired. The family likes to go camping. They love seeing movies together. Mr. Chen wants to live in a big city. Mrs. Chen wants to work in a small school. The kids want pets. Grandma wants a garden.

The Chens must decide whether to live in the city, the suburbs, or the country. They think about these things:

- What kinds of jobs can they find in each place?
- What are the homes like in each location?
- What sorts of transportation will they need in each place?
- What kinds of stores and shopping choices will they find in each place?
- What family entertainment will they find in each place?

Name _____

∽ Try It ∽

Use page 22 to help you answer these questions.

1. Pick a member of the Chen family. What would that person like about living in a city? What do you think he or she wouldn't like?

_____

_____

_____

2. Pick a different Chen family member. What would that person like about living in the country? What do you think he or she wouldn't like?

_____

_____

_____

© Harcourt

UNIT 1 Citizenship

> **Read About It** The Constitution gives American citizens many freedoms. This means American citizens are able to act and live as they choose. People living in the United States are free to travel where they want to go and to say what they think. As long as citizens follow the government's laws, they are able to enjoy these freedoms.

In the United States, people choose to live in different areas. Some people live in rural areas, while others live in cities. The act of choosing a place to live is an example of the freedoms that American citizens have.

1. What does the word "freedom" mean to you?

_____

_____

2. What freedoms do American citizens have?

_____

_____

> **Talk About It** Why is it important for American citizens to have freedom?

© Harcourt

Write About It Imagine that you are in a position of power in the government. You recently read about a country in which the citizens have little freedom. Write a letter to the leader of that country. In the letter, explain why citizens should have more freedom. Include examples to support your reasons.

_____

_____

_____

_____

_____

_____

_____

_____

_____

_____

_____

_____

_____

Mapping
Communities
Accordion Book
Unit 2

Materials needed:

*Brown paper grocery bag

*Scissors

*Pencil

*Marker

*Crayons or colored pencils

Social Studies Skills:

*Geography

*Environments

*Bridges, Buildings

Reading Skills:

*Predicting Outcome

*Draw Conclusions

*Main Idea and Details

Instructions:

1. Cut off the flap of the bag, and cut down the middle seam to open the bag up to a flat strip of paper.

2. Accordion-fold the strip into five equal parts. (You may have to trim the edges to keep all pages equal.)

Illustrations:

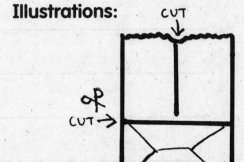

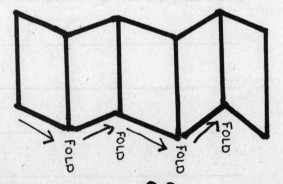

© Harcourt

3. Draw pictures of the main ideas from the chapters. Use a pencil first, then outline in marker, and color in with crayons or colored pencils.

4. Use headings from the chapters to title your illustrations.

Wait! Don't Pollute!

A readers theatre play about the importance of reducing pollution

Cast of Characters

- Narrator
- Paula
- Simon

- Mr. Wilson, Simon's father
- Brian
- Park Ranger

Setting A town park located in the eastern United States

Narrator: Paula, Brian, and Simon are walking home from school with Mr. Wilson. On the way home, they stop by the park to play for a while.

Paula: Mr. Wilson, can we go get a hot dog from the hot-dog stand? I'm starving!

Simon: Me, too! We all have our own money, Dad. Do you think it would be all right?

Mr. Wilson: I don't want you to spoil your dinner. Maybe you guys should each get a bag of pretzels. Would that be all right?

Simon: That's fine! Right, guys?

Brian: Right!

Paula: Right!

Narrator: Paula, Brian, and Simon walk to the hot-dog stand, and they each buy a bag of pretzels. They want to play, so they eat their pretzels quickly. When Paula and Simon are finished eating, they throw their empty bags on the ground. Then the two run off toward the swings. Brian places his bag in a trash can and runs to catch up with Paula and Simon.

© Harcourt

Brian: Wait up! You guys shouldn't have thrown your trash on the ground. Remember what we've been learning about pollution in school.

Simon: Don't be such a goody-two-shoes, Brian. Two bags on the ground are not going to hurt anything. Besides, my dad didn't say anything!

Brian: That's because he didn't see you do it.

Paula: Are we going to play or what? We don't have time to worry about this stuff. We have to go home in about ten minutes. Forget about it, Brian.

Brian: I guess it doesn't matter that much. Let's play!

Narrator: The kids take turns pushing each other on the swings. Meanwhile, a park ranger walks toward the kids.

Brian: Guys, look at that man coming our way. I bet he's a police officer. I told you it was wrong to throw your trash on the ground.

Paula: Relax, Brian! Let's just see what he wants.

Park Ranger: Excuse me! I'm a park ranger. I need to talk to you for a second. Are your parents here with you?

Simon: (nervously) M-my dad is here.

Park Ranger: Please go get him. He should be here for this.

Narrator: Simon calls for his dad to come over. Mr. Wilson quickly walks over to where the children are.

Mr. Wilson: Is there a problem, sir?

Park Ranger: (in a serious tone) I'm afraid there is. I saw these two (points to Simon and Paula) throw their snack bags on the ground. I wanted to talk to them about the dangers of pollution. Would that be okay?

© Harcourt

Mr. Wilson: Of course! I'm very disappointed that my son littered. I thought I had taught him better than that.

Simon: I'm sorry, Dad.

Paula: Me, too.

Park Ranger: Do you understand what pollution is? (Simon and Paula nod.) Please tell me what it is.

Simon: Pollution is littering. When I threw my bag on the ground, I created pollution.

Park Ranger: Yes, that's right. Pollution is anything that makes a natural resource dirty or unsafe to use. It may seem like a small thing to throw your trash on the ground. What if everyone just decided to put his or her trash on the ground? Think about what would happen to our world.

Simon: I never thought of it like that. I guess it all adds up.

Park Ranger: Yes, it does. But we can also think about the opposite. What if everyone picked up a piece of trash from the ground? Think about what a difference that would make.

Paula: That *would* make a difference. Simon, let's go back and pick up our trash.

Narrator: Simon and Paula run back to where they left their bags. They put them into a trash can and run back to the group.

© Harcourt

Park Ranger: Thank you for doing that. Before you go, I want to show you something.

Narrator: Mr. Wilson and the kids follow the ranger outside of the park's gates to a pond. The pond is filled with trash and litter. There is an empty trash can near the pond. The water looks so murky that they cannot see the bottom.

Brian: Ew! That water looks so gross.

Park Ranger: It wasn't always this way. Years ago, this pond had water so clear that you could see all the way to the bottom. People were able to swim in the pond, and many animals called the pond home. Now look at it. The rain has washed the trash into the pond. Dirt has made it cloudy. It's a shame.

Simon: So the pond collected all the trash people threw on the ground?

Park Ranger: Yes. Now fish and animals that lived in the pond have died. Pollution doesn't just affect people. It affects every living thing in the environment.

Brian: Wow! I wish more people would help take care of the environment. What can we do to help?

Park Ranger: Always put your trash in the right place. You can also help by spreading that message about pollution. Take what you have learned today and teach someone else.

Brian, Paula, Simon: (together) We will!

Park Ranger: My job here is done. Thank you for listening.

Narrator: The park ranger walks away. Then Mr. Wilson announces that it is time to go. Mr. Wilson and the kids walk home and think about what they learned.

The End

Simulations and Games

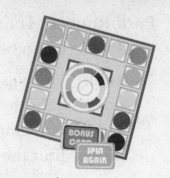

Geography Concentration   Prepare decks of
cards for students to play a variation of an old favorite.
Each deck needs 20–30 cards. Half of the deck will
present geographical terms (one per card); the other half
will give the corresponding definitions with pictures or
examples. Students play in groups of two to four. They
mix the cards and deal them face down in an array.
In turn, players turn up two cards, seeking a match. If
the player makes a match, he or she takes those cards
and gets another turn. If no match is made, the player replaces the cards and
the next player takes a turn. The game ends when all the matches have been
made. The winner is the player who has made the most matches. **GAME**

A Solution to Pollution   Introduce this simulation by discussing the
pollution problem that exists in the United States today. Remind students that
lawmakers are continually trying to find a solution to the vast amount of
pollution in the country. Divide the class into groups of about five or six. Tell
groups to imagine that the government has hired them to solve the pollution
problem. Ask groups to think of plans to help clean up the environment
in their local communities as well as in the nation as a whole. Encourage
students to think of laws that could help enforce their plan. After the
simulation, groups should discuss their plans with the class. **SIMULATION**

It's All Relative   This game will help develop students' understanding
of relative location. Divide the class into groups of three or four. Provide each
group with a map of the United States. The map should include labels for
each state and a compass rose. Have one student in each group choose a
state. Then have that person give clues that lead group members to figure out
which state the student has chosen. Explain to students that the clues should
be relative location clues. For example, if the student selected Texas, he or
she might give the following clue: "My state's location relative to Oklahoma
is south." Then each group member will take a turn guessing which state
is being described. After the group has correctly guessed the state, another
person will choose a state and give clues. Play continues until everyone has
had a turn being the clue giver. **GAME**

© Harcourt

Draw That Physical Feature   This game will help increase students' understanding of physical features. Create a stack of cards that contain names of physical features discussed in the unit. Divide the class into teams of five to seven members. Have each team select one sketcher. Give a card to the first team's sketcher, and invite the student to go to the board. Time the student for one minute while he or she draws. As the sketcher attempts to draw the word that appears on the card, the other team members must guess it in the allotted time. If they do not, give the next team a short time to figure it out. A team should receive one point each time members correctly identify a sketch. Play proceeds in this manner until all teams have had an opportunity to play. In successive rounds, each team selects a new sketcher. The game should continue until every person has had a chance to sketch or until the cards run out. **GAME**

How Would Life Change?   In this simulation, students imagine what life would be like if they lived in another region of the country. Divide the class into four groups. Assign each group one region of the country—Northeast, Southeast, Midwest, West, or Southwest. Assign each group a region other than the one in which students live. Have students discuss the characteristics of their assigned region, such as climate, physical features, and population. Then have students discuss how their lives would change. Ask questions to help facilitate discussion among the groups. Possible questions include: Where would you live? How would you get to school? What would your parents do for a living? After students have discussed as a group, bring the groups together to have a class discussion. **SIMULATION**

2 Long-Term Project

CLASS PRESENTATION: LANDFORMS EXHIBIT

Use this project to help students think in greater depth about the unique traits of different landforms.

Week 1   Introduce class 30 minutes

Materials: posterboard, reference materials, maps, atlases

Introduce the project by brainstorming with students to list all the different landforms they have learned about. Write the list on posterboard. Then help students remember the names of any landforms they may have forgotten. Add these to the list.

Week 2   Plan group 90 minutes

Materials: reference materials, Internet access

Assign small groups a different landform to investigate. Explain that their assignment is to make a model of their assigned landform. The idea is to show its key features and how it looks. Direct students to include typical plants, animals, human features, or other traits likely to be found on, in, or near the landform. Help them select a medium to use for their model, such as clay, papier-mâché, shoe box diorama, construction foam, building blocks, cardboard, or fabric. Help them get started on their planning and in the gathering of materials.

© Harcourt

Week 3 Finish Models group 90 minutes

Materials: reference books and materials, Internet access, paper, pencils, notecards

Provide time for students to complete their physical models. Then direct them to prepare a simple written display for the model they will present. Ask them to think about museum exhibits they have seen. Point out that, in most cases, along with the model or piece of art, the museum provides something in writing that gives additional information. Help students use reference materials to gather details. Have them present their ideas in the form of a poster, stand-up display, or labels that identify parts of the model.

Week 4 Have the Exhibit group 60 minutes

Materials: tables, camera (optional)

Before the presentation, have children make invitations for parents, caregivers, and other classes to visit the landforms exhibit. Help students display models and accompanying materials around the classroom. During the exhibit, have students take turns standing by their exhibits to answer questions. Encourage students to ask questions of one another and to comment on the models. Conclude by taking photographs of the exhibit and the children. Use the photographs to make a bulletin board display or scrapbook of the project.

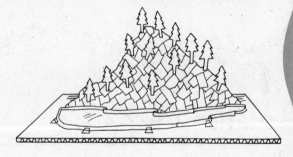

Tips for Combination Classrooms

 For Grade 2 students: Help students make an audio presentation with comments about how they made their models.

 For Grade 4 students: Ask students to include a United States map that has one or more examples of the landform highlighted with pushpins, self-stick notes, or travel photos.

UNIT
2 Short-Term Projects

The following projects can help students enhance their understanding of geography.

Chart of Regions

 group  30 minutes

Materials: reference materials, posterboard, markers

Remind students that the United States has five distinct regions. Each region contains one or more features that make it different from the other regions. Regions of the United States may differ in climate, location, culture, or economy. Divide the class into small groups. Have each group prepare a chart with four columns and five rows. Students should label the columns in the chart with the following categories: Climate, Landforms, Bodies of Water, Natural Resources. Then have students label the five rows with the names of each of the five regions found in the United States. Have groups work together to list the characteristics of each region. Encourage groups to use available reference materials. After groups have completed their charts, discuss their responses as a class.

Location Tower

individual 30 minutes

Materials: large construction paper, markers, crayons, pens or pencils

Where are you on Earth? Have students make a location tower that describes their position. Guide them to begin at the top. Have them list the most exact location they can, such as fourth desk from the door. For each level below, students give the next broader bit of information to form the tower. Have students discuss the information in their towers when they are complete.

4th desk from door
Room 3
2nd floor
Lincoln School
11 Pine Street
city of Portland
state of Maine
New England
United States of America
North America
eastern and northern hemispheres
Planet Earth
Our Solar System
The Milky Way Galaxy
The Universe

Landform Maps

 group 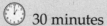 60 minutes

Materials: large construction or drawing paper, markers, pens, pencils, crayons, glue, craft sticks, any other available art materials

Landforms are everywhere, even in our own communities. Divide students into small groups and invite them to create a landform map of their community. Remind students that a landform map shows a place's main physical features. People use this type of map to learn about the geography of a place. Explain that these maps usually depict different landforms by using different colors. Tell students that sometimes landform maps are three-dimensional, meaning that the landforms appear to jump off the page. As students create their maps, encourage them to be as creative as possible and to use all available art media for their creations.

Geography and Music

class 30 minutes

Materials: tapes, records, or CDs that feature songs about geographic places or features; music books (optional); instruments (optional); sheets with lyrics (optional)

Tell students that many places are so well known for their natural beauty that songs have been written about them. State and city leaders often select a special song because it represents the location so well. Play some songs like these for students. Examples include "Oklahoma," "In My Tennessee Mountain Home," "I Left My Heart in San Francisco," "The Yellow Rose of Texas," "New York, New York," "On Top of Old Smoky," "Route 66," "America the Beautiful," and "Home on the Range." Help students learn to sing some of these songs. If possible, prepare sheets with lyrics so that everyone can sing along. As an extension, invite students to make up new lyrics to accompany the melody of a well-known song. The lyrics might celebrate interesting geographical or human-made features in your community.

Writing Projects

Use these prompts to get students writing about geography and the importance of conservation.

Landform Poems

 individual   30 minutes

Invite students to write a freestyle poem about a landform. One way to start is to have them write the name of the landform down the side of their paper, one letter per line. They use one of the letters to start each line of the poem. Taken together, the poem should give readers an image of or information about the landform. For example, these might be the first three lines of a desert poem:

Dry, dusty, and oh so hot
Each animal and plant lives a thirsty life
Staying silent and still in the midday sun. . .
E
R
T

Write an Art Review

 individual   30 minutes

Display some works of art that feature landscapes or landforms, or bookmark Internet sites to create a virtual art gallery. Examples might include Ansel Adams' photographs or paintings by Albert Bierstadt, Frederic Remington, Thomas Moran, or Thomas Cole. Invite students to write a review of a chosen work.

Human Nature

 individual   30 minutes

Remind students that our environment is not always beautiful. Some natural and human-made features can be ugly blots on the landscape. Have students write a persuasive essay about why a certain natural or human-made feature in your area should be cleaned, fixed up, torn down, or otherwise made more attractive. Remind students that the essay should describe what is wrong and then offer suggestions about why and how to make it better.

Reasons to Conserve

👤 individual   🕐 30 minutes

Remind students that conservation is the saving of resources to make them last longer. Explain to students that our natural resources will not be around forever. Land, minerals, and fuels are all scarce resources in our country today. Invite students to write an essay in which they explain the importance of conserving resources. Remind students that an essay is a piece of writing in which the author presents an argument and supports that argument with details and facts. Encourage students to use reference materials to help them.

Natural Disaster Guidebook

👥 partners   🕐 45 minutes

Explain to students that natural disasters vary according to region. For example, people who live in California are likely to experience earthquakes, while people in Florida have to deal with hurricanes during the summer and early fall. Invite students to research natural disasters that happen in their region. Have students work in pairs to write a guidebook that describes each natural disaster and suggests ways for citizens to prepare for that disaster. Encourage students to use artwork to accompany their writing.

Landform Legends

👤 individual   🕐 30 minutes

Explain to students that a legend is a story that is presented as history but is unlikely to be true. Tell students that many Native American cultures have legends that explain how the world was created. Explain that Native American legends often include unrealistic details, such as animals that can talk. Invite students to write their own legends that explain how a certain landform was first created. Have students choose a landform, such as a mountain or a plateau. Then have them brainstorm to come up with ideas for their legends. Encourage students to be as creative as possible in their writing.

Daily Geography

1. **Place**   What is a globe?

2. **Place**   What are the names of the seven continents?

3. **Location**   On which continent do you live?

4. **Regions**   Earth can be divided into halves. What is the name for one-half of Earth?

5. **Location**   What is the name for the imaginary line that is halfway between the North Pole and the South Pole?

6. **Location**   What is a border?

7. **Location**   A compass rose on a map can help you find the relative location of a place. What is relative location?

8. **Location**   What does a political map show?

9. **Location**   The latitude and longitude lines on a map are used to find the absolute location of a place. What is absolute location?

10. **Regions**   Which physical feature covers most of the middle part of the United States?

11. **Place**   What is a group of mountains called?

12. **Place**   What is the name of the main mountain range in the eastern United States?

13. **Place**   Which kind of landform lies between hills or mountains?

14. **Place**   What is a plateau?

15. **Human-Environment Interactions** Which landform would be the best place for a farm: a mountain, a plateau, or a plain?

16. **Place**   What is the name for the world's largest group of freshwater lakes?

© Harcourt

17. **Place**

Which United States river flows from Minnesota to the Gulf of Mexico?

18. **Human-Environment Interactions**

What is erosion?

19. **Place**

What is an ecosystem?

20. **Location**

What does a landform map show?

21. **Regions**

The United States is often divided into five large regions. What are the names of each of these regions?

22. **Human-Environment Interactions**

Trees, a natural resource, are used to build houses and make furniture. Are trees a renewable or nonrenewable resource?

23. **Place**

What is an environment?

24. **Human-Environment Interactions**

Which of these is a human-made feature: a plateau, a peninsula, or a highway?

25. **Human-Environment Interactions**

Which is a natural disaster: a tornado, an explosion, or thunder?

26. **Movement**

The Panama Canal cuts across the narrow strip of land that connects North America and South America. What is the main reason the canal was built?

27. **Human-Environment Interactions**

Some farmers plant crops in very dry lands and move water from other areas to water their crops. What is this process called?

28. **Human-Environment Interactions**

People often build dams in areas where flooding is common. What is a dam?

29. **Human-Environment Interactions**

What is pollution?

30. **Human-Environment Interactions**

What is conservation?

Why Character Counts

Respect

You can show respect for things as well as people. It is also important to show respect for our natural resources.

Most people in the United States have clean air to breathe. Most people have safe, fresh water to drink. This doesn't happen all by itself. We follow laws that tell us not to pollute. We obey laws that tell us not to litter. We work to keep our lakes and rivers clean.

Taking care of our natural resources is a way to show respect. Earth gives us what we need. It gives us food, water, and raw materials. We show respect by taking good care of Earth.

✓**Respect**
- **Trustworthiness**
- **Fairness**
- **Caring**
- **Patriotism**
- **Responsibility**

In Your Own Words:

What does it mean to show respect for natural resources?

_____

_____

_____

_____

_____

Name _____

Character Activity

Think about how you respect the environment by taking care of your school and its grounds. Answer the questions below. Write your response on the blank lines.

1. What natural resources do people in your school use?

_____

_____

_____

2. How do you help the environment? Explain.

_____

_____

_____

3. How might you harm the environment? Explain.

_____

_____

_____

4. Name something else you could do to help the environment. Explain how this would help.

_____

_____

_____

Economic Literacy

Scarcity

Imagine that the school cafeteria is trying out a new fruit juice to see if students like it. The cafeteria staff has asked you to help out with this experiment. They give you a carton full of juice boxes and tell you that when it is gone, there is no more. You give several juice boxes to the first few people who come through the line. You notice that you are quickly using up your supply of juice. When the next students come through the line, you give them one juice box each. After a while, you have nothing left to give. Why did this happen? You ran out of juice because your supply became scarce. You did not have enough resources to meet the needs of the people who came through the line.

In the United States, natural resources are becoming scarce. Land, fuel, and water are all resources that we are using up quickly. When something is scarce, there are not enough resources to meet people's wants and needs. Scarcity occurs only when there is a need or want for a resource, not just because there is a small amount of the resource.

When a community is faced with scarcity, the people of that community must make decisions. They need to decide how to conserve, or protect, the scarce resource so that it does not disappear. Some people place limits on the amount of a resource that can be used. Others look for ways to replace a scarce resource, such as fuel. What ways can you think of to conserve natural resources?

Name _____

Try It

Use page 44 to help you answer these questions.

1. Imagine that the cafeteria staff asks you to pass out juice boxes again. What could you do differently to make sure you do not run out of resources?

_____

_____

_____

_____

2. Think about the problem of scarcity in the United States. Choose one natural resource, and list some ways to conserve it.

Natural Resource: _____

Ways to Conserve: _____

_____

_____

_____

_____

_____

Citizenship

Read About It America has beautiful land everywhere. Some land is owned by people. It is called private land. Some land belongs to everyone. It is called public land. It is cared for by the government.

Some public land is set aside as national parks. Yellowstone National Park was the first national park. It became a park in 1872. Find Yellowstone on a map. It is located in Idaho, Montana, and Wyoming.

The National Park Service takes care of parks like Yellowstone. It keeps them clean and safe. Many people work at our parks. Some are park rangers. They help visitors, lead tours, and protect us. They care for the wildlife. They help us all enjoy our national parks.

1. Name a national park you have visited or know about. What is special about it?

   _____

   _____

2. Which national parks are closest to where you live?

   _____

   _____

Talk About It Whose responsibility is it to take care of our national parks?

Name _____

Write About It Americans do not agree about national parks and other public lands. Some believe that this land and its animals and plants should be kept safe forever.

Others disagree. They know that the land has important natural resources we all need. They want to use the minerals, forests, plant life, and water in these parks.

What do you think? Fill in the chart with your ideas.

REASONS TO *SAVE* PARK LANDS	REASONS TO *USE* PARK LANDS

Museum Capsule
Unit 3

Materials needed:
*Scraps of colored paper

*Scissors

*Glue

*2 clear plastic cups

*Clear packaging tape

*Index card

Instructions:

1. Choose a topic for the museum capsule, for example: "Landmarks in My Community" or "An Ancient Community."

2. Decide what objects best illustrate the topic. Create items to be placed in the museum capsule to form a scene about the topic.

3. Glue the items inside the cups.

Social Studies Skills:
*Community History

*Landmarks and Symbols

*Patriotism

Reading Skills:
*Cause and Effect

*Summarize

*Main Idea and Details

Illustrations:

© Harcourt

4. After the scene has been created, tape the two cups together to form the capsule.

5. Write your topic on a card to place near your capsule. Add your work to a class museum display.

TAPE

COLUMBUS'S VOYAGE TO THE NEW WORLD.

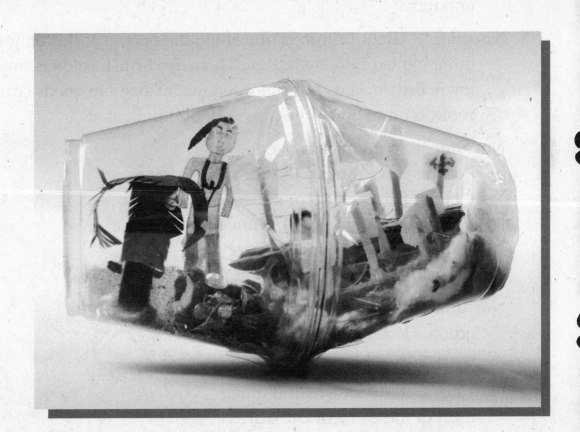

Paul Revere's Ride

A readers theatre play about the start of the American Revolution

Cast of Characters

- Narrator 1
- Narrator 2
- Narrator 3
- Dr. Joseph Warren
- Joshua Bentley
- William Dawes
- Paul Revere

Narrator 1: It is 1775. The king of England rules the American colonies. This makes many people who live in the colonies unhappy.

Narrator 2: Great Britain is punishing the people of Boston for dumping tea into the harbor. There are British soldiers in town. British ships have blocked the harbor. No goods can come in or go out. Times are very bad in Boston.

Narrator 3: A group of brave Patriots have formed the Sons of Liberty. This secret group meets to figure out what to do. Samuel Adams and John Hancock are the leaders of the group.

Narrator 1: Paul Revere is in the group. He is known as a fine horseman.

Narrator 2: Paul Revere and others meet at the home of Dr. Warren. He is also a member of the Sons of Liberty.

© Harcourt

Warren: We have trouble, men. Thousands of British soldiers march in our city. British warships have blocked the Charles River.

Bentley: The British know we have soldiers in Lexington.

Dawes: They also know about our supplies in Concord.

Bentley: The British soldiers are getting ready to attack us. But will they attack us by marching over land, or will they sail up the river?

Warren: Whichever way they go, we must let our friends in Lexington and Concord know.

Narrator 1: The Patriots come up with a plan. As soon as the British army starts to move, they will send two riders to alert the Patriots in Lexington and Concord.

Narrator 2: Warren chooses William Dawes and Paul Revere. Revere will sneak across the Charles River in a rowboat. On the other side, in Charlestown, he will be met and given a horse to ride.

Warren: Be very careful and quiet, Paul. The warship *Somerset* has 64 cannons and a watchful crew.

Revere: I will try very hard to cross safely. I'll wrap cloth around the oars to muffle their sound.

Narrator 3: The men also come up with a plan to tell Patriots in Boston about British plans. Robert Newman works at the Old North Church. He will climb up to a church window. He will hang one lantern if the British move by foot. He will hang two lanterns if they move by ship.

Warren: OK. We have our plan. Are we all agreed?

All: (excitedly) Agreed!

Narrator 1: It is Tuesday night, April 18. The British start to board their ships. Newman hangs a pair of lanterns. At 10:00 P.M., Paul Revere makes his way to the river. His dog trots along behind him.

Narrator 2: When he reaches the river, Revere finds a rowboat waiting for him. Joshua Bentley is there. So is Tom Richardson, another member of their secret group.

Bentley: You made it, Paul! But where is your cloth? And where are your spurs for riding?

Narrator 3: In his rush, Revere had forgotten both the cloth and the spurs.

Bentley: (excitedly) Wait! My friend lives nearby. I'll run over to get some cloth from her!

Revere: That's great! But what about my spurs?

Bentley: Can your dog help?

Narrator 1: Revere ties a note around the dog's neck and sends it home. The dog scampers away. So does Bentley. Revere and Richardson wait nervously. The minutes seem like days. And then they hear the dog return.

Revere: Good dog! You did it! Here are my spurs wrapped around his collar. And look, here's Bentley with the cloth! We're ready to cross the river.

Narrator 2: Silently, the three men row past the *Somerset*. They are neither seen nor heard. Soon they are safely across.

© Harcourt

Narrator 3: As planned, men wait for Revere on the riverbank. His horse is saddled and ready for the 12-mile ride to Lexington. Concord is 5 miles farther away. Revere mounts the horse and gallops off.

Revere: (to himself) I must be very careful. All the colonies are counting on me.

Narrator 1: Revere sees British scouts along the way. He avoids them. Soon he reaches Lexington. He warns the soldiers. These Patriots are called Minutemen. The Minutemen prepare to fight the British.

Narrator 2: Paul then rides off to Concord to alert the Patriots there.

Narrator 3: The next morning, the American Revolution begins. The Minutemen are ready for the British because of Paul Revere's warning.

The End

UNIT 3 Simulations and Games

Match-Up Students can use pairs of cards to match inventors with their inventions or explorers with the lands they explored. Examples might include Alexander Graham Bell and the telephone; Samuel Morse and the telegraph; Henry Ford and the automobile assembly line; John Smith and Jamestown; Pierre Laclède and St. Louis. Once students' decks of cards have been generated, they can use them to play a variety of generic games, such as "Concentration," "Go Fish," and guessing games. The goal for each game is to make correct matches. **GAME**

Town Meeting In this simulation, students hold a town meeting in a new and growing settlement. The issue to discuss is how best to use a large, vacant building in the center of town. Roles include tradespeople, shop owners, a newspaper reporter, teachers, doctors, mine workers, singers, artists, actors, police officers, firefighters, and a mayor.

Help students choose their roles. Guide them to think about creative uses that each citizen of the town might have for the available property. Tell them to list ideas for its possible uses and to prepare to speak in favor of their views. Here are some potential uses: meeting hall or community center, theater or performance space, school and library, police station and jail, bank or office building, hospital or clinic, marketplace, housing for workers.

Set a day for the town meeting. Allow time for all citizens to present their ideas in an orderly fashion and time for some give-and-take. Two citizens can take notes during the meeting. **SIMULATION**

Morse Code
Morse code sped up communications. Students today may know the sound of the Morse code SOS signal: dot-dot-dot (S), dash-dash-dash (O), dot-dot-dot (S). Post the Morse code alphabet, which is formed by combinations of short (dot) and long (dash) sounds. You can find this in an encyclopedia or on the Internet. Have students encode their names. As they become more proficient, pairs of students can try to send and receive simple one-word messages. **SIMULATION**

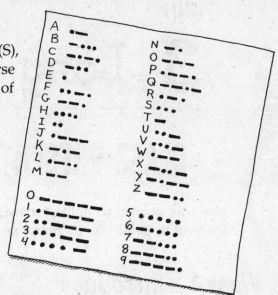

Made-Up Games
Children of all cultures, including pioneers, have always used their imaginations to come up with games, no matter what their circumstances. Invite students to share with classmates made-up games they themselves have created and played with family members, friends, or even on their own. Guide them to talk only about original games, not trademarked ones. Encourage them to think of entertainments that use only easy-to-find materials. Students can demonstrate their games to the class, or they simply can explain them. Conclude by having students prepare written rules for their games. **GAME**

American Time Line
Stretch a clothesline across the classroom to serve as a physical time line. Use labeled clothespins to mark it off in 50-year increments, starting at 1500 and ending at 2000. Select key dates in American history. Write each date on an index card, and tape it to the flat end of a separate clothespin. For example, one card might read "1776: Declaration of Independence signed." Have students hang the clothespins along the clothesline in the correct spots to form a time line of American history. Then mix up the clothespins, and challenge students to rearrange them in chronological order. **GAME**

Long-Term Project

CLASS PRESENTATION: PIONEER DAY

Use this project to help students better appreciate the pioneer way of life and to celebrate its many contributions to American culture.

Week 1   Introduce
 class   🕐 40 minutes

Materials: books on pioneer life and living skills, photographs, models

Brainstorm with students to list chores pioneers had to do every day just to survive. Guide them to think in broad terms: farm chores and care of animals, home chores, and food and water chores. Discuss, read about, and look at pictures of how to make and care for clothes, routines of hygiene and health, transportation, and toolmaking and use.

Explain that groups of students will choose and learn more about one area of pioneer life to share on Pioneer Day, to be held at the end of the unit. Projects may include creating a model of a pioneer object, home, or settlement; demonstrating a skill or craft; singing a pioneer song; telling a pioneer tall tale; making a pioneer toy; making pioneer food; or reporting on a book about pioneer life.

Week 2   Plan
 group   60 minutes

Materials: reference materials, assorted materials as needed

Guide groups of students to choose and focus the project. Help them plan a hands-on or presentation aspect based on information gathered from books and multimedia or Internet resources. Specific projects might include making and demonstrating a pioneer tool, weaving on a hand loom, making a cornhusk doll, building a model raft, explaining the value of certain farm animals, telling about pioneer health remedies, or making a pioneer bed. Obtain resource materials that provide project ideas and step-by-step instructions. Help students collect the necessary materials and supplies. Provide class time for students to work on their projects. Circulate as students work, to give them tips and advice.

Week 3   Prepare

 group 60 minutes

Materials: manila folders, markers

Have students continue working on their projects and preparing their Pioneer Day presentations. Provide manila folders students can use to make stand-up cards to identify their project. The nature of the cards will vary by project. For instance, a student who plans to make Pioneer Stew might list the ingredients. A student who will make a cornhusk doll can list the steps involved.

Week 4   Pioneer Day

 class 60 minutes

Materials: student-prepared materials, seating area, camera (optional)

Before Pioneer Day, establish an order of presentation. You may have each group share their project before the class, or students may roam to see each other's work. To add authenticity to Pioneer Day, you might ask students to wear pioneer clothing, write with charcoal, and play a pioneer game, such as hopscotch or tic-tac-toe. Photograph the presentations for a bulletin board display, an online album, or a class scrapbook. Consult *The Little House Cookbook* for simple pioneer recipes you can prepare and enjoy together.

Tips for Combination Classrooms

2-3 **For Grade 2 Students:** Have students name five things they think they would miss about modern life.

3-4 **For Grade 4 Students:** Have students make a glossary of pioneer terms associated with their project.

The following projects can help students better appreciate exploration, pioneer life, and the rise of communities.

Now That's Inventive!

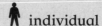 individual  45 minutes

Materials: posterboard, markers, crayons, pencils, index cards

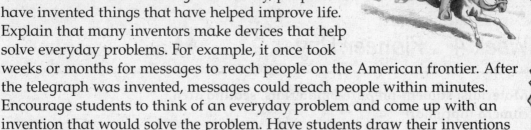

Remind students that throughout history, people have invented things that have helped improve life. Explain that many inventors make devices that help solve everyday problems. For example, it once took weeks or months for messages to reach people on the American frontier. After the telegraph was invented, messages could reach people within minutes. Encourage students to think of an everyday problem and come up with an invention that would solve the problem. Have students draw their inventions on posterboard and use the index cards to write brief descriptions. If time permits, allow students to present their creations to the class.

Compass Navigation

 group 30 minutes

Materials: simple magnetic compasses

Explain that a compass is a device used for finding directions. Remind students that when Lewis and Clark explored the Louisiana Purchase, they used a compass to help them find their way. Obtain some magnetic compasses, and show students how to use them to find the four major directions of north, south, east, and west. Then have groups use compasses to follow a simple set of directions that you have prepared in advance. The directions should be something like this: Walk 10 steps north. Shout your name. Then turn east, and walk 5 steps. Jump into the air. Then walk south 10 steps, and run in place.

Take groups outside to try to navigate with the compasses. As an extension, have students use the compasses to name the direction of landmarks from school. For instance, they might say, "The swings are found to the northeast of our classroom."

© Harcourt

Commemorative Stamps

👤 individual 🕐 45 minutes

Materials: index cards, drawing supplies, pinking shears (optional)

Display examples of commemorative postage stamps. Point out features all the stamps share, such as people, places, or events of American significance; the value of the stamp; and the abbreviation *USA*. Invite students to use the drawing materials and index cards to design a commemorative stamp about an event in American history, about a person who has brought change to the nation, or about a milestone in American technology. If pinking shears are available, students can trim the edges of the card to simulate the edges of a stamp. Have students present their stamp to the class and explain why they chose the image they did.

Language Chart

👥👤 class 🕐 30 minutes

Materials: tally table, grid paper

Point out that most early Native Americans spoke a number of different languages and dialects and could communicate with members of other tribes and clans. In the same way, many people today speak two or more different languages. Explain to students that they will help you generate a chart of the languages they and their family members speak. Begin the activity by having students interview family members to determine all the languages they speak. Have students list the languages and bring their lists to class.

Have students write each of the different languages on the board. Then arrange the languages in an order of your choosing, such as in alphabetical order or by geographic region. Work with students to make a tally table showing the results. Then help them make a class bar graph from the tally table.

Discuss the data by posing questions such as: *Which is the most common language spoken? Which is the least common language? Which language comes from farthest away?* Vary the project by focusing on languages spoken by members of your school community.

English	ЖЖ ЖЖ ЖЖ ЖЖ ЖЖ II
French	I
Hmong	II
Korean	IIII
Russian	III
Spanish	ЖЖ ЖЖ
Tagalog	III

UNIT 3 Writing Projects

Use these prompts to get students writing about exploration and communities.

Letter from an Explorer

👤 individual 🕐 30 minutes

Discuss with students how European explorers might have felt when they first saw the places we now call the Mississippi River, the Florida coast, and Canada. Talk about the descriptions they might have written to the kings and queens who paid for their travels. Then have students pretend to be the first explorers to come across your community. Have students write a letter to their imaginary sponsors. Have them tell about what they saw and whom they met.

Family Stories

👤 individual 🕐 60 minutes

Explain that early Native Americans did not use written languages. They learned about the past by hearing stories told by their elders. These stories made up the Native Americans' oral tradition. However, oral traditions apply not only to Native Americans but also to families of all backgrounds. Invite students to think of stories they have heard in their own families. Have each student choose one story to write down as a family anecdote. The story can be about something that really happened or it can be a legend or myth that has been passed down. However, it should include details that provide context and background. Also have students tell where, when, or from whom they heard their stories.

What I Admire Most

👤 individual 🕐 45 minutes

Remind students about the colonists' fight for freedom and how pioneers and explorers set up successful settlements in the Americas. Ask students to write an essay in which they express what they admire most about the ways of life during the early years of the nation. Students may focus on colonists' attitudes, beliefs, traditions, or another aspect of colonial life. Ask them to give reasons why this aspect impresses or inspires them.

© Harcourt

What a Change!

 individual   30 minutes

Remind students that all communities change over time. Change may happen overnight or over the course of many years. Invite students to think about how their own community has changed during their lifetime. Then have students think about the ways in which the community has remained the same. Ask students to write a report describing their community over time. Students should describe their first memories of the community and explain how the community is different today. Encourage students to be as detailed as possible in their report. Students who have not always lived in the same community may wish to compare their old community to their current one.

Poetic Communities

 individual   45 minutes

Remind students that they have learned about communities of long ago, such as ancient Mesopotamia and ancient Egypt. Have each student choose one of the ancient civilizations and write a poem that describes it and the contributions it has made to communities of today. Invite students to use research materials to help them find out more about their ancient communities. Remind students that not all poetry has to rhyme. Encourage students to be as creative as possible in their writing.

Biographical Sketch

  groups   60 minutes

Explain to students that pioneers are not only people who settle a new land but also people who are leaders in bringing about important changes. Point out that this unit introduced them to many pioneers, such as Dr. Martin Luther King, Jr., Elizabeth Cady Stanton, and Mohandas Gandhi. Explain that these individuals were pioneers in the area of civil rights. Have groups of students choose one of the pioneers they learned about in the unit. Ask each group to research this individual and then write a biographical sketch of the pioneer.

Daily Geography

1. **Location** — If you were visiting the Water Tower in Chicago, in which U.S. state would you be?

2. **Human-Environment Interactions** — Why were many communities built along transportation lines?

3. **Human-Environment Interactions** — Before railroads were invented, what methods did people use to travel?

4. **Movement** — Which method of transportation was invented first—the car, the train, or the airplane?

5. **Human-Environment Interactions** — What form of communication replaced the Pony Express?

6. **Place** — During ancient times, many communities grew to become great civilizations. What is a civilization?

7. **Location** — On which continent was the ancient civilization of Mesopotamia located?

8. **Location** — On which continent was the ancient civilization of Egypt located?

9. **Location** — In which country was the ancient city of Athens located?

10. **Location** — Which of the following rivers is located in Italy—the Tiber, the Mississippi, or the Amazon?

11. **Place** — The ancient empire of Mali was among the richest in the world. What is an empire?

12. **Human-Environment Interactions** — In the ancient empire of Mali, people traded gold for which two materials?

13. **Movement** — People in the ancient empire of Mali received goods from camel caravans that traveled across the land. What is a caravan?

© Harcourt

14. Place — Which landform covered most of the ancient empire of Mali—desert, mountains, or plateau?

15. Place — What is a port?

16. Human-Environment Interactions — Christopher Columbus was one of the many explorers who came to the Americas during the early 1500s. What is an explorer?

17. Movement — In which direction did Columbus sail from Spain in 1492?

18. Place — What is a settlement?

19. Location — Which city is the capital of the state north of Louisiana and south of Missouri?

20. Location — Which North American country was settled by Spain and still has a strong Spanish heritage today?

21. Place — Explorers from which country claimed much of what is now Canada?

22. Location — On which river is the city of St. Louis located?

23. Human-Environment Interactions — What do you call someone who moves from one country to live in a new community?

24. Place — The place where the Pilgrims landed became a part of which state?

25. Human-Environment Interactions — What do you call a settlement ruled by a faraway country?

26. Regions — Along which coast of the present-day United States were the 13 colonies located?

27. Movement — After the Revolutionary War, many Americans began to explore the nation. In which direction did most of those Americans move?

28. Place — After the Louisiana Purchase was made, the boundaries of the United States stretched from the east to which mountain range in the west?

29. Location — Which were the last two states to join the United States?

30. Place — How many states does the United States have in total?

Why Character Counts

Fairness

To be fair is to be honest and just. To be fair is to do what is right. Fairness means that everyone gets an equal chance.

During the 1700s, the place we now call the United States was very different. Instead of states, the land was divided into 13 colonies. The British government ruled the colonies. British lawmakers made the laws for the colonists. For a time, the colonists did not complain about British rule. Over time, the colonists began to change their minds.

The colonists felt that many British laws were unfair. The British made the colonists pay high taxes on goods. The colonists had no say in making the laws for the colonies. As a result, the British kept passing laws the colonists did not agree with. The colonists did not want to put up with this treatment anymore. They declared war on Britain. The colonists hoped to win the right to make their own laws.

- Respect
- Trustworthiness
- ✓ **Fairness**
- Caring
- Patriotism
- Responsibility

In Your Own Words:

Why did the colonists think British rule was unfair? What did they do as a result of this feeling?

_____

_____

_____

© Harcourt

Name _____

Character Activity

1. Think about British rule in the colonies. Do you think it is a good idea for one country to make the laws for another country? Is it fair? Why or why not?

_____

_____

_____

_____

_____

2. Can we bring fairness to something that has already happened? Explain.

_____

_____

_____

_____

_____

_____

Technology

Technology is all the tools people can use every day. These tools often make life easier. Computers, cell phones, and the Internet are examples of technology we use today. Technology changes the way people live and work.

Technology can help speed up the way we do things. Today, we have many ways to communicate with one another. This has not always been the case. Long ago, people had few ways of keeping in touch with others who lived far away. People sent most messages by mail. These messages took days or weeks to arrive. As a result, inventions were created that made communication faster. The telegraph and telephone both helped people spread news and other information quickly.

Technology also enables goods to be moved quickly. In the 1800s, inventions such as canals and railroads made travel faster and easier. Later, cars made it possible for people to travel on their own. People were able to drive to work. In turn, people began to move outside cities. These inventions enabled people to explore and move to new places.

Technology has helped make our lives better. For example, we are able to make goods faster. We are also able to make goods for less money. This makes it easier for us to get the things we need.

© Harcourt

Name _____

Try It

1. Make a list of the technology you use in your everyday life.

_____

_____

_____

_____

2. How has technology helped make your life better?

_____

_____

_____

_____

3. Is it possible for technology to have harmful effects? Explain.

_____

_____

_____

_____

3 Citizenship

Read About It   When our country first began, some people did not enjoy the same rights as other people. Not all people were treated equally by the law. Women had fewer rights than men had. Many African American slaves had no rights.

The Declaration of Independence helped found our country. This important piece of paper says that all men are created equal. Over time, Americans have taken this to mean that all Americans should be treated the same by the law. American heroes, like Dr. Martin Luther King, Jr., have fought to make sure all Americans enjoy the same rights.

1. How have the laws in the United States become more fair over time?

_____

_____

2. How has our understanding of the Declaration of Independence changed over the years?

_____

_____

Talk About It   Why is it important that everyone have the same rights?

Name_____

> **Write About It** Write a brief essay about some change in American life that has brought more rights to a certain group of people and helped make laws in the United States more fair.

_____

_____

_____

_____

_____

_____

_____

_____

_____

_____

_____

_____

_____

_____

_____

_____

U.S.A. A-to-Z Book

Unit 4

Materials needed:

*Blackline book page

*Markers, crayons, or colored pencils

*Scissors

Instructions:

1. Students brainstorm vocabulary words from the unit and put them in alphabetical order.

2. For a class book, students choose a letter to illustrate. They write a word on the blackline page and explain its meaning under the picture, for example: A is for anthem.

3. Students may also work in groups, with each member illustrating more than one word.

4. Tell students to combine many media on one page by drawing in pencil, outlining in marker, and coloring with crayons or colored pencils. They may wish to use glitter or gel pens and other art media, if available, to "jazz up" their page.

Social Studies Skills:

*Local Government

*Leaders

*National Government

Reading Skills:

*Categorize

*Summarize

*Main Idea and Details

Illustrations:

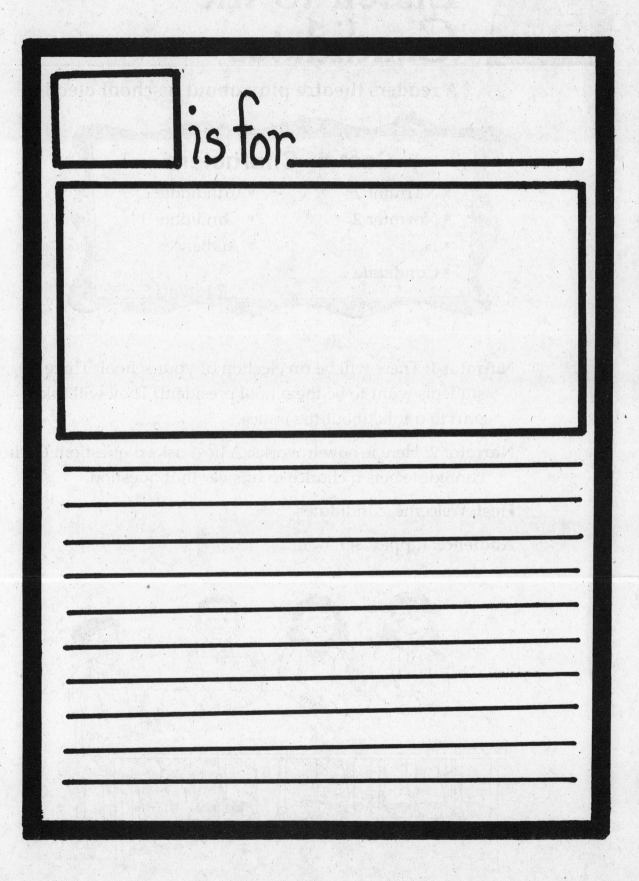

is for _____

Listen to the Candidates

A readers theatre play about a school election

Cast of Characters

- Narrator 1
- Narrator 2
- Host
- Candidate 1
- Candidate 2
- Candidate 3
- Audience

Narrator 1: There will be an election at your school. Three students want to be the school president. They will take part in a talk about the issues.

Narrator 2: Here is how it works: A host asks a question. Each candidate gets a chance to answer that question.

Host: Welcome, candidates.

Audience: (applause)

© Harcourt

Host: Here is the first question. Candidate 1, why do you want to be school president?

Candidate 1: Our school is already good. I want to make it even better. I like working with others in a group. Groups work best when people share ideas. Together, we can work to make our school a great place.

Host: Candidate 2, why do you want to be school president?

Candidate 2: I think I will make a great school president. I care about things. I like making decisions. People listen to me. I'm a good leader. And I am hardly ever absent.

Host: Now it's your turn, Candidate 3. Why do you want to be school president?

Candidate 3: I want to be school president a lot. I like people. I like to make plans. I like to go to meetings and say my ideas. I have a lot of good ideas.

Narrator 1: All three candidates have now answered the first question. Now the host asks the second question. This time, Candidate 2 answers first.

Host: Candidate 2, what is one school problem you will work to fix?

Candidate 2: We need better food in the lunchroom. And that's not all. I want to make sure that they don't put soda machines or candy machines in our school, like they did in my sister's high school. We already eat too much junk food.

Host: Now it's your turn, Candidate 3. What is one school problem you will work to fix?

Candidate 3: The biggest problem I see is that we don't have enough time away from school. I'll argue for shorter school days and longer holidays. If I am elected, I will also ask teachers to give less homework over the weekend.

Host: Candidate 1, let's hear your thoughts now. What school problem will you work to fix?

Candidate 1: I think we should make better use of our school. I hope we can have more after-school activities, homework help, library time, and sports games.

Narrator 2: Now the host asks the third question. This time, Candidate 3 gets to answer first.

Host: Candidate 3, tell us what makes you the best choice for school president.

Candidate 3: I believe that I am the best choice for president. I make friends easily. People like me. I'm a good listener, and I am polite. I'm funny, too. Vote for me so I can make you proud.

Host: Now it's your turn, Candidate 1. Tell us what makes you the best choice for school president.

Candidate 1: As I see it, a vote for me is a vote for you. I will work for you in every way I can. Kids should have their voices heard. I will try to start a school newspaper so kids from all grades can share their good ideas. I have ideas for getting kids of different ages to work and play together.

Host: For our final comment, we turn to Candidate 2. Tell us, Candidate 2, what makes you the best choice for school president?

Candidate 2: I want to do a good job. I am honest and hardworking. You can count on me. I care about many issues. I promise that I will get the job done.

Host: That ends our talk with the candidates. Thank you all very much. We all look ahead to Election Day. Let's thank our three candidates for their time.

Audience: (applause)

Narrator 1: You have heard all three candidates answer the host's questions. You have heard three different points of view.

Narrator 2: You have also heard ways in which their views are alike.

Narrator 1: Now it is time to vote for school president.

Narrator 2: Who will you vote for? Which views did you like the best? The choice is yours.

The End

UNIT 4 Simulations and Games

Trial In this simulation, students hold a mock trial to get a better sense of the workings of the court system. Present a well-known fictional situation as the reason for the trial. For example, try "The Case of the Stolen Broom," in which Dorothy is tried for stealing the broomstick of the Wicked Witch of the West in *The Wizard of Oz*. Or try "The Case of Mistaken Identity," in which Prince Charming accuses Cinderella of pretending to be rich. In "The Case of the Lying Boy," Pinocchio could be tried for telling lies.

Discuss typical trial processes. Point out that a trial is conducted calmly and formally and that people take turns speaking. Arguing and calling out is not allowed. Explain the function of each member of a trial: the judge and jury hear the evidence, the plaintiff tells the reasons for accusing the defendant, the defendant defends his or her actions, the lawyers ask questions, the bailiff keeps things running smoothly, and the observers listen but may not participate.

After you select a case, help students choose roles. Guide them to think about what each character might say and how each would behave. Have them jot down notes in preparation.

Set a day for the trial. Arrange classroom furniture to suggest a courtroom. Have the bailiff and the judge explain the rules and enforce fairness. Remind students to act as their characters would and to listen politely when others speak. Conclude by talking about the process, the verdict, and the whole experience. **SIMULATION**

States and Capitals To play this game, you will need a large outline map of the United States and a few small beanbags.

In this game, players take turns tossing a beanbag at the map. To earn points, they must identify the state on which the beanbag lands and the capital of that state. A player earns one point for naming the state and one point for naming its capital. Variations may include having one person toss the beanbag and another person identify the state and capital. **GAME**

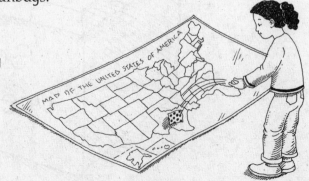

Word Jumble

Provide a word jumble to reinforce the vocabulary of government and citizenship. Give the letters of each word in scrambled order, with one letter highlighted in each word. The highlighted letters will form a bonus word in each set. Post a word bank to help students spell the words correctly as they unscramble them. Finally, have students unscramble the key letters to spell another word about government or citizenship. **GAME**

Jumbled Word	Correct Term
red leaf	federal
pride tens	president
line cote	election
dejug	judge
corcymade	democracy
cotton in suit	constitution
jaryomit	majority
	= FREEDOM

Jumbled Word	Correct Term
ryuj	jury
vexiecute	executive
grisht	rights
setta	state
uglisterale	legislature
ucotr	court
songresc	congress
	= JUSTICE

Government Quiz

Students working in teams can play a variation of a well-known television quiz show. Prepare a set of cards that give answers based on terms and ideas from the unit. When each card is shown, teams, in turn, must pose a question whose answer is the word or phrase on the card. Examples include *legislative* (*Which branch of government makes laws?*), *amendment* (*What do you call a law added to the Constitution?*), and *capitol* (*What do you call the building that houses the government in a capital city?*). **GAME**

© Harcourt

UNIT 4 Long-Term Project

THE FOUR FREEDOMS MURAL

Use this project to build students' appreciation of some of the basic freedoms that Americans enjoy.

Week 1 Introduce

class   45 minutes

Materials: images of President Franklin D. Roosevelt, the Norman Rockwell paintings of "The Four Freedoms"

Introduce the project by explaining to students that many government leaders fight to uphold the rights and freedoms of American citizens. Explain that former President Franklin Delano Roosevelt is an example of a leader who fought for the freedom of citizens. Tell students that Roosevelt made a famous speech to Congress on January 6, 1941, after World War II had begun in Europe. Among the ideas in his speech, Roosevelt described the "Four Freedoms." These freedoms were the basic rights he believed mattered to most Americans. Invite students to guess what these freedoms might be.

Next, display and discuss the Norman Rockwell images of Roosevelt's Four Freedoms: freedom of speech/expression; freedom of worship; freedom from want; and freedom from fear. Tell students that Rockwell was a popular artist whose works are still shown today. He was best known for painting magazine covers. "The Four Freedoms" appeared in four weekly editions of the magazine *Saturday Evening Post* in 1943. Rockwell's original paintings were taken on tour all over the United States, where people paid to see them. The money that was raised—$132 million—went to support government efforts to protect our country.

Tell students that together the class will work to create an updated version of "The Four Freedoms," with images that reflect life in the United States today. Each group will be responsible for one part of the mural, which will be assembled and presented together.

© Harcourt

Week 2   Plan group 60 minutes

Materials: butcher paper, assorted art supplies, old magazines, glue, scissors

Divide the class into four groups. Assign each group one of the four freedoms. Distribute assorted art supplies, including markers, crayons, and old magazines from which to snip related images, and make a large workspace available. Encourage groups to talk about the kinds of images that would represent the freedom they have been given to depict. Groups can decide whether to make one large image, as Norman Rockwell did, or make a collage/montage of images that convey the idea. Give students time to get started on the mural.

Week 3   Finish the Mural group 60 minutes

Materials: butcher paper, assorted art supplies, collected images, lined paper

Have groups work to complete their images. Ask students to prepare a simple statement to introduce the mural. In the statement, they should name the freedom, say why it is important, and tell how Americans can enjoy this freedom in their daily lives.

Week 4   Display the Mural group 30 minutes

Have each group present what its part of the mural shows and answer questions from the rest of the class. Invite other classrooms and students' parents or guardians to view the mural as well.

Tips for Combination Classrooms

 For Grade 2 students: Have students name some freedoms they would add to the mural if they were to expand it.

 For Grade 4 students: Have students determine how many years ago Franklin D. Roosevelt made his speech and Norman Rockwell created his paintings. Have them prepare a simple biographical sketch for each of these historical figures.

Short-Term Projects

Use these projects to help students explore, examine, and respond to some aspects of community cooperation.

Becoming a U.S. Citizen
 class 45 minutes

Materials: index cards

Invite a visitor to address the class on the topic of why, when, and how he or she chose to become a citizen of the United States. The visitor can be a friend or family member of one of your students, a community leader, or anyone else who is willing to be interviewed by the class. Prepare students by talking about the kinds of questions they might like to ask the guest. Have them write their questions on index cards. Sort through the cards to eliminate duplicate or inappropriate questions. Invite students to read their questions aloud to the guest, who may answer them. Conclude the activity by writing a class thank-you note to the guest.

> Why did you decide to come to the United States?

Rhymes of America
 group 30 minutes

Materials: *A Book of Americans* **by Stephen Vincent Benet**

Select some poems about famous Americans, freedom, or patriotism. One good resource is the poems Stephen Vincent Benet wrote with his wife, Rosemary, in 1933. Or select works by contemporary poets or songwriters on American themes. Give each group one poem to read together. Have them practice reading the poem aloud slowly, clearly, and with feeling. Guide students on how to present a poem as a unison choral reading. Allow ample time for practice. Then invite each group to present its poem to classmates.

Safety Walkabout

 class   60 minutes

Materials: clipboards, paper, pencil

Take students on a walk around your classroom, your school, and your neighborhood in search of evidence of rules, laws, or practices that keep citizens safe. Have students make notes of what they notice, which might include signs, fences, color coding, special lighting, guardrails, or access ramps for people with disabilities.

Back in the classroom, list the evidence students have gathered. Guide them to look for ways to sort the information, such as whether the rules or laws are for safety, convenience, cleanliness, or organization.

Ideas for Voting

 group   30 minutes

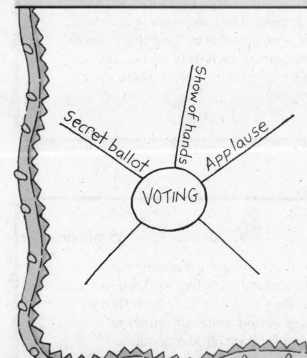

Materials: chart paper

Brainstorm with students some ideas involved in holding elections. Capture the main ideas of the discussion in an idea web. For example, components of one web might include ways to vote (i.e., show of hands, written ballot, applause), open voting vs. secret ballot, formal vs. informal elections, and so on. Or students might create a flowchart that shows the steps involved in the election process. Have students work in groups to generate different graphic organizers about voting. Post the results, and invite students to add ideas as they continue to learn more about elections.

Writing Projects

Use these prompts to get students writing about citizenship and government.

Hero Sketches

 individual   30 minutes

Invite students to select a person—real or fictional—whose character traits they admire. Have them write a character sketch of that person that highlights his or her best qualities and that supports their view that this person ought to be regarded as a hero or as a valuable citizen. When the sketches are completed, invite volunteers to read them aloud.

Campaign Speech

 individual   45 minutes

Explain to students that candidates for public office seek ways to help voters learn about who they are and what they believe. The campaign speech is a common way for candidates to get their points across to the public. Have students pretend to be candidates for public office, such as governor, mayor, or county judge. Invite them to write a short campaign speech. Then, invite volunteers to give their speeches before the class.

Election Posters

 partners   45 minutes

Tell students that government agencies and private groups often print up informational posters to help new voters. Have students, working in pairs, create election information posters. They might include such things as drawings of voting booths, definitions of voting terms, or names of candidates and the offices they are running for. Help students gather pertinent information from websites and social studies reference books. Post the finished products around the classroom.

Research a State Bird

individual   **30 minutes**

Help students write a simple research report on our national bird, the bald eagle, or on the bird that represents your state. Have them begin by thinking of five useful questions they could answer, such as these: *What is the name of the bird? What does it look like? How big is it? Where does it live? What does it eat? What sort of nest does it build? What does its call/song sound like? How many eggs does the mother lay at a time?* Then help students find information to answer the questions about the bird. Have them write their report in a question-and-answer format and include drawings or photographs of the bird.

Citizenship Poem

individual   **30 minutes**

Invite students to write freestyle poems about citizenship. One way to begin is to have them write a key term, such as *democracy* or *volunteer*, down the side of their paper, one letter per line. They use each letter to start each line of the poem. The poem itself should give readers an image of or information about the key word. For example, here is a poem about freedom that you can share with students:

> **F**or life, for liberty, for happiness,
> **R**ural people, urban people, young or old,
> **E**very person hopes to be free. We want
> **E**qual chances, fair choices, and
> **D**reams of a better life. We are
> **O**ne nation, a land of
> **M**any people, many ideas, and one important goal.

Classroom Bill of Rights

individual   **30 minutes**

Remind students that the Bill of Rights lists the basic rights that belong to all citizens of the United States. Explain that the government cannot take these rights away. Ask students to think about the rights they have in the classroom, especially the ones the teacher cannot take away. Invite students to create a classroom bill of rights. Encourage students to propose their own list of rights and provide a brief explanation of why students should be guaranteed those rights. If time permits, have students share their work with the class.

Daily Geography

1. **Location**   What is the capital city of Indiana?

2. **Location**   Rosa Parks and other African Americans held a bus boycott in the city of Montgomery. Montgomery is the capital of which state?

3. **Location**   What city is the capital of Maryland?

4. **Location**   The nation's laws are made at the U.S. Capitol Building. Where is this building located?

5. **Place**   What is a county?

6. **Regions**   What is the name of the city where the main government of a county is located?

7. **Place**   Which of these cities is a state capital?
Denver
Los Angeles
Philadelphia

8. **Place**   Which two capital cities have the state names in their own names?

9. **Location**   Which two neighboring states have Bismarck and Pierre as capitals?

10. **Location**   Which capital city is farther west—Concord, New Hampshire, or Montpelier, Vermont?

11. **Location**   If you were in Boise, in which state would you be?

12. **Movement**   In which direction would you travel if you were going from the capital of Maryland to the capital of Virginia?

13. **Movement**   Through which state capitals could you pass if you were traveling from Virginia straight to Georgia?

14. **Location**   Which capital city is located on an island?

15. **Place**   What are the names of your state and your county?

© Harcourt

16. Place   Which two states share no borders with other states?

17. Location   In which direction is Tallahassee, Florida, from Jefferson City, Missouri?

18. Location   Which state borders Nebraska to the south?

19. Location   Which state borders Alabama to the north?

20. Location   Which state borders Ohio to the west?

21. Location   Which state borders Arizona to the east?

22. Location   Between which two states is Washington, D.C., located?

23. Place   Each of the 50 states has its own capitol building, where lawmakers meet to make state laws. Where are state capitol buildings normally located?

24. Location   In which city and state is the Liberty Bell located?

25. Location   The Lincoln Memorial, the Vietnam Veterans Memorial, and the National World War II Memorial are all located in which city?

26. Location   Francis Scott Key wrote our national anthem while watching a War of 1812 battle. Near which city and state did this battle take place?

27. Location   Which country touches the United States on the south?

28. Location   Which country forms the northern border of the United States?

29. Location   On which continent is the country of Bhutan located?

30. Place   What is the name of the mountain range located in Bhutan?

Why Character Counts

Patriotism

Patriotism is a feeling of pride in one's country. People can show patriotism through their actions or words. Francis Scott Key is an example of a person who used words to express patriotic feelings. During the War of 1812, Key watched the British attack a U.S. fort. The battle lasted into the night. When the battle ended, it was too dark for Key to see who won. However, the next morning, when he saw the American flag flying high in the sky, all his doubts were erased. The images Key saw that night moved him to write our national anthem—"The Star-Spangled Banner."

- **Trustworthiness**
- **Respect**
- **Responsibility**
- **Fairness**
- **Caring**
- ✓**Patriotism**

Today, patriotism is alive and well all over the world. You can be patriotic without writing a national anthem. You are patriotic when you care about your country. You are patriotic when you take pride in your country. You are patriotic when you are a loyal citizen.

In Your Own Words:

How do you show patriotism?

_____

_____

_____

Name _____

Character Activity

Answer the following questions about how we show patriotism. Write your answers on the blank lines.

1. When do we say the Pledge of Allegiance to our flag? What does it mean to say the Pledge?

   _____

   _____

   _____

2. When do we sing "The Star-Spangled Banner"? What is this song about?

   _____

   _____

   _____

3. Write a short poem that tells why you are proud of the United States.

   _____

   _____

   _____

   _____

Economic Literacy

Public and Private

Where do you go to buy food? You probably go to a supermarket or maybe to a local grocery shop. Supermarkets and other stores that sell food or other goods are owned by individuals, by families, or by groups of people. Most stores are private businesses.

If you want to borrow a book, where do you go? You probably go to the public library. Libraries are free. They are for everybody to enjoy. They are provided for our communities by our government. When people pay taxes, some of the money goes to keep libraries open and filled with books. Having libraries is a public service. The workers who take care of our roads also offer a public service.

© Harcourt

Name _____

Read the description of the goods and services listed in the table. Decide whether each is a public or private good or service. Then check the correct column. If goods or services can be both public and private, then check both columns.

Make a ✔ to identify the kind of goods or services.

Goods and Services	Public	Private
1. Mailing letters and packages		
2. Building highways, tunnels, or bridges		
3. Setting up and caring for parks or zoos		
4. Caring for the sick		
5. Searching for lawbreakers and missing people		
6. Offering protection from crime		
7. Building houses and stores		
8. Putting in streetlights and traffic signs		
9. Organizing parades		
10. Holding a book fair or a crafts festival		
11. Providing job training		
12. Providing an education		
13. Selling cars and trucks		
14. Giving driving tests and driver's licenses		
15. Selling toothpaste and shampoo		
16. Offering day-care services		
17. Recycling plastic, glass, metal, and paper		
18. Presenting the news		
19. Creating television programs		
20. Providing transportation		

© Harcourt

Citizenship

Citizens who are 18 years old or older get to choose our leaders. They elect our President and Vice President every four years. Voting for our leaders is an important right. It is an important part of citizenship.

Even if you are not old enough to vote, you can learn about your leaders. You can read about them in newspapers, in magazines, and online. You can learn about the beliefs of our leaders. You can find out what they have done. Getting used to learning about our leaders will help you when you are old enough to vote.

1. How old do you have to be to vote in the United States? In which national election will you be able to vote for the first time?

_____

_____

2. Should you care who gets elected even if you are too young to vote? Why or why not? Explain.

_____

_____

Voting is one of the key responsibilities that citizens have. What do you think it means to be a responsible voter?

© Harcourt

Name _____

1. Who is the President of the United States?

   _____

2. Who is the Vice President of the United States?

   _____

3. To which political party do the President and Vice President belong?

   _____

4. What are the names of the two United States senators from your state?

   _____

5. Who is the governor of your state?

   _____

6. Who is the representative to the United States House of Representatives from your area?

   _____

7. Does your town or city have a mayor? If so, who is your mayor?

   _____

8. How do leaders help shape a community?

   _____

Hero Box
Unit 5

Materials needed:

*Scissors

*Cereal box

*Drawing paper

*Colored pencils, markers, or crayons

*Glue

*Construction paper

Social Studies Skills:

*American Heroes

*Folk Heroes

*Immigrants

Reading Skills:

*Summarize

*Point of View

*Main Idea and Details

Instructions:

1. Measure four pieces of drawing paper against the four sides of a cereal box. Cut the pieces of paper to fit each side of the box.

2. Draw lines for your writing and boxes for your pictures on each piece of paper. On the page for the back of the box, draw a wheel-like circle, as shown to the right.

3. Choose an American hero or folk hero to illustrate. Draw your hero in pencil on the paper for the front of the box. Then outline your drawing with black marker and color it, adding background.

Illustrations:

4. Tell the story of the hero on the paper for the back of the box. Fill in characteristics of the hero and summarize what he or she did.

5. On one of the narrow pieces of paper, draw the person and tell why he or she is your hero. On the other, draw yourself and tell how you learned about the person.

6. Cut construction paper to fit the four sides of the box. Glue it on to cover up the writing about the cereal. Then glue your paper onto the box, and decorate the construction paper around them.

A New Life

A readers theatre play about immigration

Cast of Characters

- Narrator 1
- Narrator 2
- Istvan
- Miklos
- Dan
- Mr. Moore

Narrator 1: It is the very early 1900s. Istvan and his brother Miklos must work. They cannot go to school. They need to help support their family.

Narrator 2: Times are tough in Hungary and in other countries of eastern Europe.

Narrator 1: Jobs are hard to find. But Istvan and Miklos are lucky. Their uncle is a painter. So they work for him and learn to paint.

Narrator 2: The boys work nearly every day. The work is hard, the hours are long, and the pay is low.

Narrator 1: Istvan and Miklos want to do more to help their family. As they work, they hear stories about life in the United States. People say the streets there are paved with gold and everyone is rich.

Narrator 2: The boys believe that they will be able to find good jobs in America. When the boys get older, the family leaves Hungary. They board a ship going to the United States.

Narrator 1: As the ship approaches Ellis Island, the boys feel excited. They cannot wait to begin their lives in the United States.

Narrator 2: But times are tough in the United States, too. Work is hard to find. The streets are not paved with gold. In the United States, the boys and their family are as poor as they were back in Hungary. They live in a crowded city in a tiny apartment. There is not enough money.

Narrator 1: But Istvan and Miklos have a trade. They can paint. Every day, they go out looking for work. They have little luck. Many U.S. citizens dislike immigrants and do not want to hire Istvan and Miklos.

Narrator 2: The boys begin to give up hope. Then one day, Istvan comes home smiling.

Istvan: Guess what? I found us a job! We start tomorrow!

Miklos: That's wonderful! Where is the job? What does it pay?

Istvan: We're working for a man who is painting a big house on Fifth Avenue.

Miklos: That's great, but how much will we be paid?

Istvan: Not much, I'm afraid. One dollar each for every day we work.

Miklos: That's all?

Istvan: I'm afraid so. But it's better than nothing, and nothing is what we're earning now. Let's just go there and do our best.

Narrator 1: That night, their mother comes home with a sack of bread, meat, and butter. She wants the boys to be well fed for their job the next day. The boys go to bed early. They wake up excited to get to work. Their mother packs a big lunch for them to take with them.

Narrator 2: Istvan and Miklos take their lunch and leave for work. They ride the train. Then they walk three blocks to Fifth Avenue. The house is huge and grand! They ring the big brass doorbell. A butler lets them in.

Miklos: What a house! It must have at least 20 rooms.

Istvan: Look how high the ceilings are. And look at all the fancy details we'll have to paint.

Narrator 1: The man who hired the brothers enters the room.

Dan: Hello, boys. I want you to go to the second floor and paint the master bedroom. Be careful. There are many pieces of fine art and furniture there. Mr. Moore expects your best work.

Narrator 2: The young painters enter the huge room. It is fancy! It will take lots of work just to move the heavy furniture away from the walls.

Istvan: Come, Miklos. Let's move this big dresser first. Watch the mirror!

Narrator 1: With great effort, the painters carefully move it a few feet. Then Miklos spots something on the rug where the dresser had been. He bends over and picks it up.

Miklos: My goodness, Istvan, look at this! It's a $500 bill!

Istvan: Wow! I've never seen so much money. This is more money than we could earn in a year!

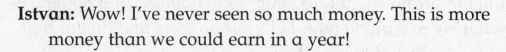

Miklos: What do we do? Do we keep it? I mean, would Mr. Moore know? He is so rich he probably wouldn't miss it. It would help us so much. We could buy mother a winter coat. And we could buy father new shoes. Or should we turn it in?

Istvan: Mr. Moore might not miss it. He might not even know it was lost. Still, it's wrong to keep it. The money is not ours, Miklos.

Miklos: (*sighing*) You're right, my brother. Let's give the bill to Dan.

Narrator 2: The young painters look for Dan. But before they find him, Istvan and Miklos bump into Mr. Moore. He smiles at them.

Mr. Moore: How's it going in there, young men?

Miklos: Mr. Moore, sir, we found something under your dresser.

Istvan: Yes, sir, here it is—a $500 bill.

Narrator 1: Istvan hands over the bill. Mr. Moore takes it and looks at it closely. For a moment, the brothers stand in silence. Then they begin to turn and walk away.

Mr. Moore: Wait. I want you to know how thankful I am. You did the right thing.

Istvan and Miklos: Thank you, sir.

Mr. Moore: I have something for you. A regular job. You two have earned my trust. I want you to work in the paint department in my main store. I'll pay each of you $500 a year. How does that sound?

Narrator 2: That sounded just fine to Istvan and Miklos.

Narrator 1: The boys had done the right thing, and they were rewarded. Although the streets of the United States were not paved with gold, the boys believed that the land was full of opportunity!

The End

Simulations and Games

New National Landmarks In this simulation, students hold a mock meeting of a committee that is planning a new national landmark celebrating the multiculturalism of the United States. Encourage students to think of topics to cover during the meeting, and invite them to suggest ideas to discuss. Record their responses on the board. Ideas to explore might include the location of the new landmark, its design, how to represent all the cultures of the nation, methods of construction, how to finance construction, the hours of operation, and slogans to advertise the monument. Assign roles to students. Roles may include meeting leader, secretary, and committee members.

Set a time for the meeting. Arrange classroom furniture to suggest a meeting room. Have the meeting leader open the meeting and call on people to speak in turn. Remind students to listen politely when others speak. Encourage discussion and give-and-take, as might occur in a public meeting. Encourage students to provide their opinions of the positive and negative aspects of the project. **SIMULATION**

Category Spin Prepare a round spinner of five equal-sized sections. Label the sections National Landmarks; National Holidays; Cultural Holidays; Religions in the United States; and Written and Oral Traditions.

Each team consists of a pair of students, and two pairs play against each other. To play, a player from Pair A spins the pointer. Pair B must name an example that fits the category indicated. For example, if the pointer lands on National Landmarks, an appropriate answer might be the Statue of Liberty. Teams record correct responses on a tally sheet divided into categories that match the five sections. As the game goes on, players may not repeat answers. Play continues until one team is stumped and cannot give a correct response. **GAME**

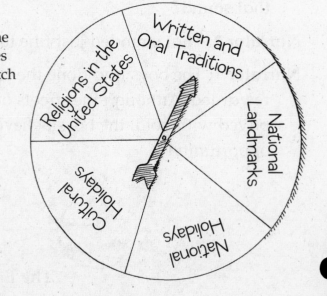

© Harcourt

What's That Term?   Divide the class into groups of four or five. Make up a pack of index cards that contain vocabulary words and other important words and concepts from the unit. Each group should have its own pack of word cards. Have each group select a clue giver. Each clue giver selects a card from the pack and gives clues about it, without saying any part or form of the word written on the card. As the clues are given, the remaining group members take turns guessing the term or concept that is being described. After the term or word has been guessed correctly, another group member becomes the clue giver. Play continues for as long as time allows or until the cards run out. **GAME**

True or False?   Divide the class into groups of four or five. Give each group two cards—one with the letter *T* and the other with the letter *F*. Write the letters boldly so that they can be read from a distance. Before starting the game, compile a list of true/false questions based on material from the unit. To begin the game, ask the class one of the true/false questions, and give group members one minute to discuss their response. After the minute has passed, ask one member of each group to hold up the card displaying the group's answer. Award one point to each group displaying the correct answer. Award no points for incorrect answers. The game proceeds in this manner until you have asked all the questions or time runs out. The group with the most points at the end wins. If there is a tie, ask one final true/false question. The first team to respond correctly wins. To vary the game, award 1 extra point to the first group that can explain why an answer is either true or false. **GAME**

Coming to America   In this simulation, students will play the roles of immigrants who travel to the United States during the late 1800s and early 1900s. Divide the class into groups of four or five. Invite students to imagine they are immigrants on a ship traveling to the United States. Have the groups hold discussions on topics such as why they are coming to the United States, who they are traveling with, how they feel about leaving home, and what they expect life in the United States to be like. Facilitate group discussions by asking questions such as these: *What country are you coming from? What job do you hope to have in the United States? What has your journey on the ship been like? What do you expect to happen when you get off the ship?* After students have held small-group discussions, have a class discussion. **SIMULATION**

5 Long-Term Project

MULTICULTURAL PAGEANT

This project invites students to explore the diversity of the citizens of the United States and to discover the customs and traditions of different cultural groups.

Week 1 Introduce class 45 minutes

Introduce the project by discussing the meaning of *multiculturalism.* Tell students that together the class will prepare a pageant that features multicultural ideas and symbols. Explain that in this project, students will create a Gallery of Flags. Each pair of students will take part in two ways: by making a flag that represents the culture they are investigating and by singing a cultural song, telling about an important cultural symbol or holiday, dressing as a person from that culture, or performing a skit representing an important event from that culture's history.

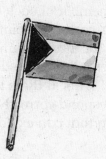

Week 2 Gallery of Flags partners 60 minutes

Materials: large sheets of butcher paper, crayons, markers, paints, brushes, photographs, reference materials as needed

Divide the class into pairs. Assign each pair a culture to investigate. Examples include Native American, West African, Maya, Chinese, and Thai. Give each pair a large sheet of butcher paper on which to create a culture flag. Explain that the flag can be a replica of a flag from a country associated with the assigned culture, or it can include symbols and drawings that represent the culture. Provide reference books, paintings, and photographs students can consult. Have students label their flags and write one or two sentences describing them.

Week 3   Prepare partners   90 minutes

Materials: reference materials as needed

During this week, pairs should work on their second contributions to the Multicultural Pageant. Students may need help in choosing a cultural song, selecting a poem about an important cultural event, doing research about a cultural symbol or holiday, planning a simple skit, selecting a cultural food to prepare, or designing the costume of a person from that culture. Allow time for students to practice until they can present their contributions clearly to the group.

Week 4   Hold the Pageant   class   45 minutes

Materials: student-prepared materials, camera (optional)

Prior to the presentations, you may wish to invite guests, such as family members, students from other classes, and the principal, to come to the pageant. Before the pageant, help students plan an order for the events or activities. Make a poster or program that presents this order. On the day of the pageant, welcome guests, and have guides take guests through the Gallery of Flags and tell about the flags on display. Have each pair present its second contribution by singing, reciting, speaking, performing, or serving. If possible, take photographs of the events, and conclude the pageant by displaying them.

Tips for Combination Classrooms

2-3 **For Grade 2 students:** Have each student write a paragraph that explains what he or she likes best about the culture he or she investigated.

3-4 **For Grade 4 students:** Have each student include more detailed information, such as the capital city, population, geographic location, and climate, about the country he or she is presenting in the Gallery of Flags display.

5 Short-Term Projects

Use these projects to help students explore, examine, and respond to cultural groups, landmarks, and events that Americans share.

Mapping Population

 partners   45 minutes

Materials: reference materials, Internet access, enlarged outline map of your state (with major cities labeled), drawing supplies

Remind students that a population map can show where most people in a particular community or region live. Explain to students that places have different population densities, or numbers of people living in areas of certain sizes. Assist students as necessary to use reference materials and the Internet to find the populations of major cities in your state. Have pairs use different colors to represent cities with different-sized populations. After students have completed their map, have them compare their map to those of other pairs. Ask them to point out and explain differences between the maps.

Landmarks Pamphlet

 partners   60 minutes

Materials: reference materials, Internet access, crayons or markers, paper, pencils, large map of the U.S., yarn, pushpins

Brainstorm with students to list some American monuments and landmarks. Invite pairs of students to work together to create an informational pamphlet about the chosen site. Ideas include a travel brochure, map or geographical guide, or picture book about the place. Help students gather information from websites, travel books, encyclopedias, or other print materials. Display the completed projects on a large map of the United States. Use yarn and pushpins to connect the pamphlets with the geographical location of the sites they feature.

Immigration over the Years

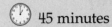 partners · 45 minutes

Materials: construction paper, ruler, markers, reference materials

Have partners research the numbers of people who immigrated to the United States between 1900 and 2000. Have them make a bar graph that reflects how the number of immigrants changed through the decades. If needed, remind students that a decade is a period of ten years. Suggest that they label the years along the bottom of the graph and the population numbers along the left side of the graph. Explain that the years should begin with 1900 and increase by ten-year intervals to the year 2000. Encourage students to share their charts with one another's. If time permits, you may wish to have students write sentences to explain changes in the numbers of immigrants entering the country from year to year.

Happy Holidays!

 individual 30 minutes

Materials: reference materials, large construction or drawing paper, art supplies, index cards

Remind students that people around the world express their cultures with holidays and celebrations. As a class, create a list of holidays that are celebrated around the world. Then have each student research a holiday that another culture celebrates. Invite students to create a poster that shows how people in the culture celebrate that holiday.

Encourage students to use available reference materials in order to learn more about the holiday they chose. After students have completed their posters, have them write a short explanation of the holiday on an index card. The explanation should answer the questions *Who? What? When? Where? Why?* and *How?* Display the posters in the classroom. Invite students to view each other's posters during free time.

5 Writing Projects

Use these prompts to get students writing about culture and traditions.

Flag-Folding Directions

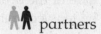 partners   30 minutes

Tell students that there is a formal, proper way to fold an American flag so that it forms a triangular bundle with the blue field of stars showing. Using flags, towels, scarves, or rectangular pieces of fabric, show students how to fold the flag. Then divide the class into pairs and challenge them to write a set of instructions for this task. Guide them to give the steps in order so that someone who has never folded the flag could follow along.

Praising Diversity

 individual   30 minutes

Remind students that the United States is multicultural society. This means that people from different cultures and ethnicities live and work together. Invite students to think about what multiculturalism means to them. Ask students to write an essay that answers the following two questions: *What does multiculturalism mean to me? Why is multiculturalism important to the American culture?* Encourage students to be as descriptive as possible in their writing.

Lady Liberty Literature

 individual   45 minutes

Tell students that there are many books about the Statue of Liberty. Titles include *The Story of the Statue of Liberty* by Betsy Maestro; *Looking for Liberty* by Harvey Stevenson; *Liberty's Journey* by Kelly DiPuccio; *Liberty!* by Allan Drummond; *Lily and Miss Liberty* by Carla Stevens; *A Picnic in October* by Eve Bunting; and *I Was Dreaming of Coming to America* by Veronica Lawlor. Have children select and read a book about the Statue of Liberty or a book in which Lady Liberty plays a role. It can be fiction or nonfiction. Have them write a personal response to the book.

Fables

 individual  60 minutes

Explain that people often share their cultures through literature. Remind students that people of some cultures use fables to express their ideas about life and the world. Fables are stories in which animals speak and act like humans and which usually share some kind of moral, or lesson, with the reader. Introduce students to Aesop's fable "The Tortoise and the Hare" to show the moral tradition of fables. Invite students to write and illustrate their own fables that teach a lesson.

What's Your Custom?

 individual 45 minutes

Begin this activity by reminding students that all cultures have customs and traditions. Tell students that families often have unique customs and traditions, too. Have students think about customs and traditions their families share. Tell students that these can include an activity that takes place during a special holiday or a tradition involving everyday life. Invite students to write descriptive accounts about a family tradition or custom. Students can write a story about a time when they took part in the tradition, or they can simply describe the tradition. If time permits, have students share their stories with one another.

Class Cookbook

 group 30 minutes

Have students gather recipes that originated from other regions or countries. Students may use the Internet or library resources to find these recipes, and they may also ask family members to provide recipes. Direct students to write down the recipes they find. Point out that recipes begin with a list of ingredients and then give step-by-step instructions to prepare the dish. Then ask them to add a sentence about the country or region where this recipe originated. When all students have turned in recipes, compile a class cookbook.

5 Daily Geography

1. **Regions**   In the past, many people living in the Appalachian region had a culture different from that of people living in other regions of the United States. What was the main reason for this?

2. **Movement**   Between 1890 and 1920, millions of new immigrants arrived in the United States. What is an immigrant?

3. **Movement**   Which part of the United States did most immigrants from Asia reach first?

4. **Movement**   Which ocean did immigrants cross to come to the United States from Europe?

5. **Movement**   In what direction would you travel if you were coming from South America to the United States?

6. **Movement**   Immigrants traveling from Africa to the United States are moving in which direction?

7. **Location**   In what United States location did most immigrants from Europe arrive?

8. **Location**   On the West Coast, many immigrants were welcomed to the United States at Angel Island. In which body of water does Angel Island lie?

9. **Location**   Most of the immigrants entering the United States today come from what country?

10. **Place**   During the 1900s, many African Americans took part in the Great Migration. What does it mean to *migrate*?

11. **Regions**   During the Great Migration, African Americans moved from the South to which regions of the United States?

12. **Human-Environment Interactions**   Since the 1970s, many people from the northern United States have moved to the Sun Belt. Why have so many people chosen to live in the Sun Belt?

13. **Place**   Different areas have different population densities. What is population density?

14. Place   In which place—a city, a small town, or a rural area—would the population density likely be greatest?

15. Place   Which part of your state has the greatest population density?

16. Place   The Adams Morgan neighborhood in Washington, D.C., is home to people from many different ethnic groups. What is an ethnic group?

17. Location   On which of the five Great Lakes is the city of Cleveland, Ohio, located?

18. Place   The United States has many national landmarks. What is a landmark?

19. Place   The United States received the Statue of Liberty as a gift. What country gave the statue to the United States?

20. Location   In which state can you find the Statue of Liberty?

21. Place   In which state is Mount Rushmore National Memorial located?

22. Place   The *kalungu* is a type of drum used in African music. From which country does this drum come?

23. Location   In which present-day country is the ancient city of Tikal located?

24. Place   On March 17, many people in the United States celebrate St. Patrick's Day. From which country did this holiday come?

25. Place   Cinco de Mayo is a holiday that was first celebrated in which country?

26. Place   On September 16, people in Mexico celebrate their independence from what country?

27. Place   About how many countries does the continent of Africa have?

28. Place   About how many countries does the continent of Europe have?

29. Movement   In which direction would you travel if you were going from the United States to Brazil?

30. Place   In which country is the festival Carnaval held?

© Harcourt

Why Character Counts

Responsibility

Responsibility means to know and do what is right. You can count on a responsible person. That person can be trusted. A responsible person does the right thing, even if it is hard.

People have a responsibility to help their communities. John Chapman knew this, and he did something about it. In the region where Chapman lived, it was hard to bring food in from other areas. He helped hundreds of settlers set up apple orchards. Many settlers were able to have fresh fruit in their diets, thanks to him.

Most people are not able to repeat John Chapman's actions. They do not have the time or resources to plant apple orchards around the country. Still, every person can make a difference in the community. There are many ways to do this. Even small actions can help. For example, you can show responsibility by putting trash into a trash can.

- Trustworthiness
- Respect
- ✓ **Responsibility**
- Fairness
- Caring
- Patriotism

In Your Own Words:

Why do people have a responsibility to help their communities?

_____

_____

_____

_____

Name _____

Character Activity

What responsibilities do you and your classmates have? In what ways must you be responsible at home and in school? What chores are yours to do? Do you care for pets? Do you set or clear the dinner table? How else do you help around the house or in the neighborhood? In what other ways are you responsible?

Now be a reporter. Talk to three different students in your class to learn about the ways in which they are responsible. Listen to what they say. Take notes. Use your notes and ideas to answer the following questions.

1. What responsibilities do children my age have at home?

_____

_____

_____

2. What responsibilities do we have when we are in school?

_____

_____

_____

3. Are there other ways to show that we are responsible? What are they?

_____

_____

_____

_____

© Harcourt

5 Economic Literacy

Competition

Competition is like a contest. In a running competition, runners work to win a race. Businesses can also face competition. When two businesses in the same area offer the same good or service, they are competing against each other.

In Chamblee, Georgia, for example, many cultural groups live and work together. Immigrants make up a large part of the city's population. The city has more than 100 businesses owned by immigrants. Some of these businesses provide the same good or service. This means that the businesses are in competition with one another.

Competition makes businesses work harder. Businesses try to make their goods or services seem better than the competition's. Sometimes, businesses lower prices to gain customers. Other times, they try to get attention by making eye-catching advertisements.

Competition can be good for business. When a business offers lower prices, more customers are likely to buy its products. Having many customers is always good for business. Competition is also good for consumers. Businesses that are in competition with one another work hard to make their products the best they can be. As a result, consumers get better products for lower cost. However, sometimes, competition can be bad for business. Some businesses have a hard time keeping up with the competition. This may force some businesses to close.

© Harcourt

Name _____

Use page 110 to help you answer these questions.

1. Imagine that you have just started a new business. A week later, another business opens that sells the same product. What things can you do to beat the competition?

_____

_____

_____

_____

_____

2. Two businesses are located on the same street. Both businesses sell the same product. Business A lowers its price. Business B cannot afford to lower its price. More customers go to Business A. What will happen to Business B? Explain.

_____

_____

_____

_____

© Harcourt

5 Citizenship

Read About It All people living in the United States have rights. The Declaration of Independence says that citizens have rights that cannot be taken away. All citizens have the rights to life, liberty, and the pursuit of happiness. This means that no one can take away your life, freedom, or chance to be happy.

The idea of life, liberty, and the pursuit of happiness led many immigrants to the United States. They wanted to have opportunities they would not have anywhere else. Some hoped to find more freedoms. Others wanted better jobs. Immigrants hoped that having the rights to life, liberty, and a chance at happiness would help them achieve better lives.

1. What are the three rights that the Declaration says cannot be taken away?

_____

_____

2. Why did the idea of having these rights lead many immigrants to the United States?

_____

_____

Talk About It Why was it important to include the rights to life, liberty, and the pursuit of happiness in the Declaration of Independence? What might happen if these rights were taken away?

Name _____

> **Write About It**   Write a play in which two immigrants are discussing their reasons for coming to the United States. Include in the play the idea of the rights to life, liberty, and the pursuit of happiness.

_____

_____

_____

_____

_____

_____

_____

_____

_____

_____

_____

_____

_____

_____

Product Packet
Unit 6

Materials needed:

*Drawing paper

*Construction paper

*Glue

*Crayons, markers, or
 colored pencils

*Scissors

*Tape

Instructions:

1. Cut two pieces of construction
   paper a little larger than the
   drawing paper. Tape three of the
   edges. Then glue the drawing paper
   to the front and back.

2. Illustrate the front of the packet
   with a product or a natural
   resource. Draw it with pencil, outline
   it with a black marker, and color
   it in.

Social Studies Skills:

*Resources and Products

*Selling Products

*Consumers

Reading Skills:

*Summarize

*Main Idea and Details

*Generalize

Illustrations:

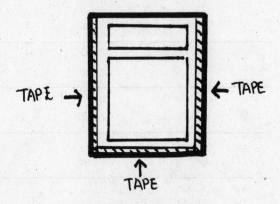

3. On the back of the packet, write in facts about the product or natural resource.

4. Make a display about the product or natural resource out of construction paper and slide it into the packet.

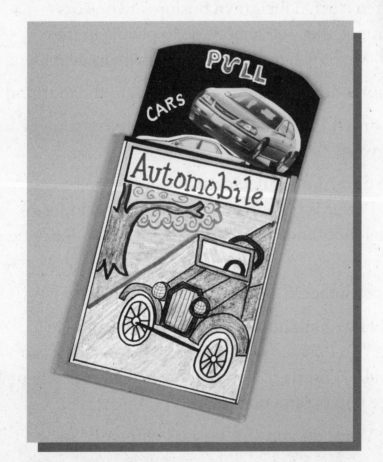

All Business

A readers theatre play about a child-owned business

Cast of Characters

- Narrator
- Alma
- José
- Porter
- Mr. Sanchez
- Customer

Setting: A lemonade stand on a neighborhood street

Narrator: It is early in the morning on a hot summer day. José and his friend Alma are setting up their lemonade stand. The two children started their own business two years ago. Each summer, they sell lemonade to people in the neighborhood. Mr. Sanchez, José's dad, is there to help them.

Alma: Man, it's hot today, and it's just 8 o'clock in the morning.

José: (wiping his brow) I know! That means more consumers for us. I can't wait!

Narrator: As José and Alma talk, Porter listens to their conversation. Porter is a younger child who lives in José's and Alma's neighborhood. José and Alma do not notice he is there.

Porter: What's a consumer?

José: Hey, Porter! How long have you been standing there? (Porter shrugs.) To answer your question, a consumer is a person who buys a product. You will be a consumer when you buy a nice cup of lemonade!

Alma: (laughing) What do you say, Porter? You want some lemonade?

© Harcourt

Porter: Sure, but I don't have much money.

José: Well, our lemonade is only 25 cents a cup.

Porter: That's it? I can pay that. (Porter gives Alma a quarter.) Why are you selling the lemonade for so little money?

Alma: We want more people to visit our stand. Even though it's a hot day, we still have competition from the store down the street.

Porter: What's competition? You mean like a race?

José: Sort of. The store down the street sells lemonade and many other products. We have to do what we can to get consumers to buy our lemonade. When we make our prices lower, we hope that more people will buy our product.

Porter: That makes sense.

Mr. Sanchez: (grinning) José! Alma! Customers are coming. Pay attention!

José: All right, Dad.

Porter: I'll let you guys work. I'll be back later.

Narrator: Porter walks away just as the first customer arrives.

Alma: Good morning. Would you like a cup of lemonade?

Customer: Yes, please! I'd like two cups.

José: That will be 50 cents.

Customer: What a great deal! I'll be sure to come back here again.

Alma: Thanks! Have a good day!

Narrator: The customer leaves, and suddenly ten more appear. Alma and José are very busy for the next few hours. In the late afternoon, Porter shows up again. Alma and José are sitting behind the stand with tired looks on their faces.

Porter: You two look beat. Did you sell a lot of lemonade?

Alma: We did. We sold 100 cups. We made a huge profit.

Porter: What's a profit?

José: (sighing) A profit is the money left over after all the costs of running our business have been paid.

Porter: But what does that mean? I don't understand.

Alma: Mr. Sanchez, Porter wants to know what *profit* means. Can you help us explain?

Mr. Sanchez: I'd be glad to. Porter, it costs money to run a business. José and Alma have to pay for the supplies for the lemonade. They have to buy the ingredients to make the lemonade and the cups to pour it into. Does that make sense so far?

Porter: (nodding his head) Yes, it does.

Mr. Sanchez: When Alma and José sell a cup of lemonade, they have to use the money they earn to pay for the supplies. After they pay for those supplies, any money left over is their profit. It's for them to keep.

Porter: Now I understand. Thanks, Mr. Sanchez.

José: Alma, let's clean up. Our supplies are running low, and it's getting late.

Narrator: Alma and José clean up the stand. Porter pitches in, and the work is soon done.

José: Thanks, Porter. I'd say that you definitely deserve a wage today. Before you ask, a wage is the money you earn at work. Since you helped us, you should get some of the money we earned. (José hands some money to Porter.)

Porter: Wow! Thanks! I've never had a real job before. Do you think I could help you out again sometime?

Alma: I think that might be fine. You could help us clean up. You could also help us advertise.

Porter: I know what it means to advertise. You want me to make posters and flyers that get people to come buy lemonade.

José: Exactly!

Porter: I can do that.

Mr. Sanchez: Porter, now that you are going to be making money, you must learn to budget your money. A budget is a plan for spending and saving money.

Porter: I already know that I want to save all my money. Then later I can buy the things I want.

Mr. Sanchez: That's a good plan, Porter.

Porter: I have to go. I'll see you guys at work tomorrow.

Narrator: Porter runs off, and Mr. Sanchez, José, and Alma go home. They are going to rest so they will be ready for another day of selling lemonade.

The End

UNIT 6 Simulations and Games

Mail-Order Shopping In this simulation, students pretend to order the goods needed to set up a simple one-room cabin in the woods for two people. Tell them to imagine that the cabin has a fireplace for heat and cooking, an ice chest for keeping food cold, and a pump that brings cold water inside. The cabin has two windows, one door, and a wooden floor. It has no electricity. There is a garden patch in the backyard.

Explain to students that long before there were shopping malls, discount stores, or e-commerce, people could order what they needed from mail-order companies such as Montgomery Ward or Sears. Catalog companies sold goods at fair prices and delivered them to their customers.

Obtain all-purpose catalogs from general retailers. Divide the class into small groups. Give each group a catalog, a basic order form, a calculator, and an imaginary budget of $4,000. Tell them to use the money wisely to set up a working household. Guide them first to think of the most important needs. Instruct them not to use this budget for food or clothing, but only for durable goods—items used over and over, such as furniture, cooking equipment, and blankets. Have participants list items first and then rank them by importance or necessity. Then they fill out their order and calculate the total. **SIMULATION**

Product Possibilities Divide the class into small groups. Explain that each group will think about an abundant natural resource found somewhere in the world, such as lumber, aluminum, oil, wheat, cattle, or cotton. During a five-minute time limit, each player works independently to list as many items as possible that could be manufactured or produced from that natural resource. When time is up, each player reads aloud the items on his or her list as group members consult their own lists. The group then creates a master list of each natural resource mentioned by someone in the group. Instruct groups to list natural resources only once even if more than one person in the group mentioned it. The group with the greatest number of natural resources wins the game. **GAME**

© Harcourt

Barter Day In this simulation, students learn about this form of economic transaction by bartering with classmates. Invite students to bring to class two or three simple items they would like to barter. Send a note home to inform parents or guardians of this activity and to request their guidance in helping children select suitable items. Remind students to select items that have some value but that they are willing to part with if they can come to an agreement with another person. Tell students to ask themselves the following questions when choosing items to barter: *Is this item mine to trade? Am I willing to barter it away? What value does it have? Who might want it? How will I decide on a fair trade?*

Set the day for the bartering. Have students display their items in advance so that everyone can see what is available. Then allow time for students to negotiate, haggle, or otherwise work out terms for the exchanges. Guide students to think creatively to reach fair trades. Conclude by talking about the experience. Extend by discussing the pros and cons of bartering. **SIMULATION**

Trade Treasure Hunt Remind students that goods and products Americans use come from all over the United States and from other countries. In this activity, students do a trade treasure hunt at home, and then use their findings in a classroom game.

Ask students to do the preliminary step at home: read labels of items around their household—foods, clothing, durable goods, books, toys, etc.—to identify a variety of places of origin. Students can invite family members to help. Tell students to write each product and its place of origin on an index card. Afterward, they should organize their cards alphabetically by place-name.

In class the next day, form small teams. Within a team, students share cards to form a master deck of all places of origin they found. Now teams are ready to play to earn points. To play, teams take turns reading from one of their cards a place of origin and the product it produced. For example, a student might say, "South Korea was the source of a television." In turn, each other group looks at its cards for a product that also comes from South Korea. If no other team has South Korea as a location, the group scores a point. Play continues in turn until a team scores seven points. As an alternative, have teams place different-colored pushpins on a world map to highlight every country from which they found a product in their trade treasure hunt; the team with the greatest number of pushpins wins. **GAME**

© Harcourt

UNIT

6 Long-Term Project

COMMUNITY MARKETPLACE

Use this project to highlight economic concepts introduced in the unit.

Week 1 Introduce   class   45 minutes

Materials: advertisements, reference materials, chart paper, markers

Introduce the project by having students generate a list of words and phrases that explain what makes a good business. On a sheet of chart paper, record the words or phrases students name. Explain that students will be opening a marketplace in the classroom. The classroom will become a free market economy, in which students become entrepreneurs and develop their own businesses. Divide the class into six teams. Each team is responsible for building a booth to represent its business. Tell students that the businesses they create are intended for consumers their age. Have students brainstorm the types of products and goods children their age would like to buy. Record their responses on the chart paper.

Week 2 Plan    group   60 minutes

Materials: paper, Internet access

For this part of the project, each team is responsible for developing a plan for its business. Have students think about the kind of business they would like to have. Guide students by having them answer the following questions: *What goods or services will our business provide? How will we get people to buy our goods? What will we do if faced with competition?* Then give students time to plan their booths and to discuss whether to include things like advertisements, pamphlets, examples/illustrations of their products, and descriptions of the products. Remind students that each group member must be responsible for some aspect of the project, and assist groups as needed.

© Harcourt

Week 3 Create  group ⏱ 60 minutes

Materials: drawing paper, art supplies, Internet access

Give students time to make the materials they need for their booths. As students develop their advertisements, remind them that the purpose of an advertisement is to attract customers. Advise students to use bright colors and bold lettering. If possible, invite older students who are skilled at computer graphics to help your students draw up their pamphlets and advertisements.

Week 4 Marketplace Day ⏱ group ⏱ 90 minutes

Materials: student-prepared materials, display area

Allow students a few minutes to set up their booths and display their advertisements and pamphlets. Then give students time to visit one another's booths. Designate three groups to be the consumers and three groups to be the entrepreneurs. Have the entrepreneurs stand near their booths and the consumers visit each booth. Ask the entrepreneurs to explain their business to the consumers, describe the type of product they are selling, and explain why people might buy the product. After all the entrepreneurs have presented, have the groups switch roles and repeat the process. After every group has presented its business idea, have a class discussion to recap the project.

Tips for Combination Classrooms

2-3 **For Grade 2 students:** Have students write help-wanted ads for their businesses. Tell students that in writing an appropriate ad, it helps to think about the characteristics that workers for their companies would need to have.

3-4 **For Grade 4 students:** Have students create a chart of all the resources they will need to start their business. Remind them to include natural, human, and capital resources.

© Harcourt

UNIT
6 Short-Term Projects

Use these projects to help students explore trade, commerce, and communication in your community.

Market Research

 class  60 minutes

Materials: clipboards, pencils, paper

Take the class on a trip to a local supermarket or grocery store. Look for evidence of local, national, and international commerce. Direct students to the produce and dairy sections of the store. These departments specialize in perishable goods that must be replenished regularly. Arrange in advance to speak with a store employee who can answer questions about the sources of perishable merchandise. Direct students to record all the different places goods come from. Back in the classroom, list all the different locations and help students find them on map.

Budget Your Allowance

 individual 30 minutes

Materials: paper, pencils

Challenge students to create a sensible budget for a weekly allowance of an amount you determine. Point out that there is no right or wrong budget because each person can make choices about how to spend his or her money. However, emphasize that it is important to stick within the limits of a budget. Invite volunteers to share their budgets and to explain the reasons behind some of their choices.

© Harcourt

High-Tech Mural

👤👤👤 group   🕐 45 minutes

Materials: butcher paper, catalogs and magazines, glue, markers

Brainstorm with students a list of high-tech equipment that has become part of our lives. Look at the list with students to find categories to sort the items under, such as: tools, gadgets, health supplies, toys, communications devices, sports equipment, or entertainment gear. Divide the class into small groups and assign each group a different category. Students will create a mural of technology related to their category. Students can collect pictures, advertisements, brochures, or other related images from newspapers, catalogs, magazines, or product packages. Provide a long piece of butcher paper to form the background for the mural. Have students post their contributions and add labels or data to make the mural more informative.

Survey of First Jobs

👤 individual   🕐 45 minutes

Explain to students that most adults will work at more than one kind of job during their working life. The jobs they do when they are older may be very different from the jobs they did when they first entered the workforce. Have students interview a parent or guardian to find out about the first paying job that person ever had. Tell students to ask their subjects to describe the job, how they found it, what they did, and what the working conditions were like. Remind students to take notes.

When students come together again in class, invite them to share what they found out. Guide them to look for common features of early employment experiences.

Writing Projects

Use these prompts to get students writing about economics.

Job Wanted

 individual 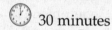 30 minutes

Tell students that some people look for work by advertising in the newspaper or online. To do this, job seekers list the kind of job or work they seek and describe why they are best suited for it. Invite students to write a "job-wanted" ad. They can select a real job or an imaginary job. Then they write a persuasive paragraph about why they are the best candidate for the job. Have them write the ad *without* including their real name. Post the ads on a bulletin board. Invite classmates to peruse the ads to see who they might be interested in hiring, if they had a job to offer.

A Biography

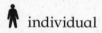 individual 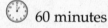 60 minutes

Help students select and research a businessperson for a short biography. Some examples are: Wally Amos, Andrew Carnegie, Walt Disney, Henry Ford, Bill Gates, Paul Newman, Ben (Cohen) & Jerry (Greenfield), Alice Waters, Madame C. J. Walker, and Oprah Winfrey. Suggest that students answer in their biography questions such as: *Who is/was this person? What is/was this person's greatest accomplishment? How did this person help or change the United States?*

Kid Power

 class   45 minutes

Show the 1992 film *Newsies*, which portrays the 1899 strike of New York City newsboys against the unfair labor practices of publishers Joseph Pulitzer and William Randolph Hearst. Discuss the film with students. Then ask them to write an imaginary letter to Mr. Pulitzer or Mr. Hearst, giving their opinion of the business practices that upset the newsies.

© Harcourt

Business Resources

 individual    60 minutes

Remind students that businesses need resources in order to make products and to provide services. Explain what those resources are—natural resources, human resources, and capital resources. Have each student choose a business in the community to study. Invite students to use available materials to learn more about the business. Students may do research on the Internet or visit the business with family members. Have students write a report in which they describe the business and list the resources it needs. After the reports are written, invite volunteers to share the information in their report. To vary the assignment, have students draw up a plan for their own business and write a report telling the resources they would need to start it.

What If . . .

 individual   30 minutes

Explain that inventions, such as the computer and the telephone, have changed the way people do business. Advances in transportation have also helped move goods quickly. Have students imagine how life would change if all the world's modern technology suddenly disappeared. Ask students to think about how this would affect business. Invite students to write a story explaining what businesses would do if all the technology disappeared. Encourage students to be as creative as possible in their writing.

Commercials

 partners   45 minutes

Discuss with students the purpose of commercials: to get people interested in buying a particular product. Ads can be serious, fact-filled, or funny, but all try to make people remember a product or service. Invite students to create a commercial to get consumers to buy a particular product. The product can be something real (for example, a toy, movie, restaurant, pet, or food) or imaginary (for example, a new invention or impossible travel). Have them envision the ad airing on radio or television for no more than 30 seconds. Guide partners to think of an idea for the commercial, write the copy, and practice delivering it. Ask volunteers to share their commercial with the class.

6 Daily Geography

1. **Location**   Joanne Miller runs a cleaning business in Chicago. In what state is the city of Chicago located?

2. **Human-Environment Interactions**   Some businesses use raw materials to make products and provide services. What is a raw material?

3. **Human-Environment Interactions**   Businesses often depend on human resources to make goods. What is a human resource?

4. **Place**   What information does a land use and products map show?

5. **Place**   What does the key on a land use and products map include?

6. **Place**   Name two products that people in your state grow or make.

7. **Location**   Why might people who live in cold climates buy fruit from other regions during the winter?

8. **Movement**   In the United States, barges are often used to ship goods from place to place. What is a barge?

9. **Movement**   Transportation has made international trade possible. What is international trade?

10. **Movement**   Each day, imports arrive in the United States. What is an import?

11. **Movement**   The United States sends many exports to other countries. What is an export?

12. **Movement**   Name two exports of the United States.

13. **Movement**   What are two countries that export rice?

14. **Movement**   The United States imports most of its cars from which country?

15. **Movement**   Some countries are known for large exports of one product. What country is one of the world's main exporters of tea?

© Harcourt

16. Movement Name one product the United States imports from Canada.

17. Human-Environment Interactions In 2005, Hurricane Katrina destroyed many communities in the United States. Which states were most affected by Hurricane Katrina?

18. Movement Today, a lot of business is done through e-commerce. What is e-commerce?

19. Movement In the past, people often exchanged goods by bartering. What is bartering?

20. Regions In which region of the world is the euro used as a form of money?

21. Location People once used cowrie shells as money. Name two countries that used cowrie shells as money.

22. Location In ancient times people began to use coins as a form of money. In what country did people first use coins?

23. Location In 1792, the United States Mint began making coins. In which U.S. city was the first United States Mint located?

24. Location The United States Bureau of Engraving and Printing makes our paper money. Where is one of the United States Bureaus of Engraving and Printing located?

25. Human-Environment Interactions The United States has a free market economy. What is a free market economy?

26. Location Kid Blink was a famous newsie who fought against unfair practices by the newspaper companies. In which city did Kid Blink work?

27. Human-Environment Interactions During a drought, crops such as wheat become scarce. What does it mean for something to be scarce?

28. Location What city is the main business center in Japan?

29. Location On which continent is the country of Mozambique located?

30. Location What two oceans surround the continent of Africa?

© Harcourt

Why Character Counts

Trustworthiness

To be trustworthy means other people can trust you. It means that other people can depend on you to do what you are supposed to do. People who are trustworthy tell the truth. A person who is trustworthy is someone worth your trust.

Trustworthiness is important to business in many ways. You can count on a trustworthy business. You can trust its products will be good.

Businesses want workers who will do a good job. They want workers with experience. Businesses also want workers who are trustworthy. They want workers who will do their job when they are supposed to. They want workers who will tell the truth. Trustworthiness is very important to businesses.

✓ **Trustworthiness**
- **Respect**
- **Responsibility**
- **Fairness**
- **Caring**
- **Patriotism**

In Your Own Words:

How do people show they are trustworthy? Explain.

_____

_____

_____

© Harcourt

Name _____

Character Activity

Pick a job that you would like to have one day. Think about that job for a moment. Then answer these questions about trustworthiness at work. Write your answers on the blank lines.

1. In what ways could you show your trustworthiness at this job?

_____

_____

_____

2. In what ways could your employer show that he or she is trustworthy?

_____

_____

_____

3. How could your customers or clients show that they are trustworthy?

_____

_____

_____

UNIT 6 Economic Literacy

The Internet

Today, many people use the Internet to communicate with other people. They also use the Internet to shop. People even use the Internet to make deposits in saving accounts at the bank. Often, using the Internet saves time and work. But people need to be careful, especially when they use the Internet to buy goods or make deposits in the bank.

An adult you know might use the Internet to buy goods, like books. Often the only way to buy a good over the Internet is to use a credit card. Many adults do this. But before they send their credit card information through the Internet, they first need to be sure their information will be safe. They need to make sure the correct business receives their information. They need to make sure they can trust the company.

Name _____

Try It

Interview one of your parents or guardians about the Internet. Ask the questions below and fill in the answers.

1. How much do you use the Internet?

_____

_____

2. Do you use the Internet to shop, bank, or communicate?

_____

_____

3. How has the Internet changed your life? How has it improved your life?

_____

_____

4. What problems do you run into when you use the Internet?

_____

_____

5. Why do you need to be careful when you use the Internet?

_____

_____

Write a summary about what you found out on a separate sheet of paper.

Read About It As a citizen of the United States, you have many job opportunities. You might work in a bank or in a hospital. You might be a firefighter or a teacher. You can work in any area that interests you. Your opportunity to get a job does not depend on where you come from, your skin color, your religion, or whether you are a boy or a girl. The Constitution protects your right to work in any area you please.

The Constitution was signed on September 17, 1787. People now celebrate this date as Constitution Day. On this day, people remember why the Constitution is important. They think about the ideas included in the Constitution, such as equality, freedom, and opportunity. Constitution Day reminds us to be thankful for the opportunities we have.

1. What protects your right to go after any job opportunity that interests you?

_____

_____

2. What is Constitution Day? Why do people celebrate it?

_____

_____

Talk About It Many jobs require that you get a certain amount of education before you can begin. Why is it important to go to school before getting a job?

© Harcourt

Name ______________________________

Write About It What is the job that most interests you? Why? How could you improve your chances of doing this job? Explain.

Social Studies Journal

The single most important thing I learned was . . .

Something that confused me or that I did not understand was . . .

What surprised me the most was . . .

I would like to know more about . . .

Sources I can use to find answers to my questions are . . .

The part that made the greatest impact on me was . . .

Reading Guide

Questions I have before reading				New questions I have after reading
Question **1**	Question **2**	Question **3**	Question **4**	Question:
				Question:
Summary of what I learned after reading that answers my questions				Other interesting information I learned while reading
Question **1**	Question **2**	Question **3**	Question **4**	
General summary:				My reaction to what I read:

Current Events

Summary of an important event:

WHO:

WHAT:

WHEN:

WHERE:

HOW:

Where did it take place? Draw a map.

Why?

What was the cause?

What was the effect?

Comparison

This event is similar to . . .

Prediction

What do I think will happen next?

Personal Reaction

My reaction to the event:

Visual Literacy

Explain what is happening in the artwork.

Explain the mood of the artwork.

Describe the artwork.

Explain what the artist is trying to show you.

© Harcourt

Main Idea and
Supporting Details

Supporting Detail

Supporting Detail

➡ **MAIN IDEA** ⬅

Supporting Detail

Supporting Detail

Fact and Opinion

Fact	Opinion
✓ **Fact**	✗ **Opinion**
✓ **Fact**	✗ **Opinion**
✓ **Fact**	✗ **Opinion**
✓ **Fact**	✗ **Opinion**

© Harcourt

Causes and Effects

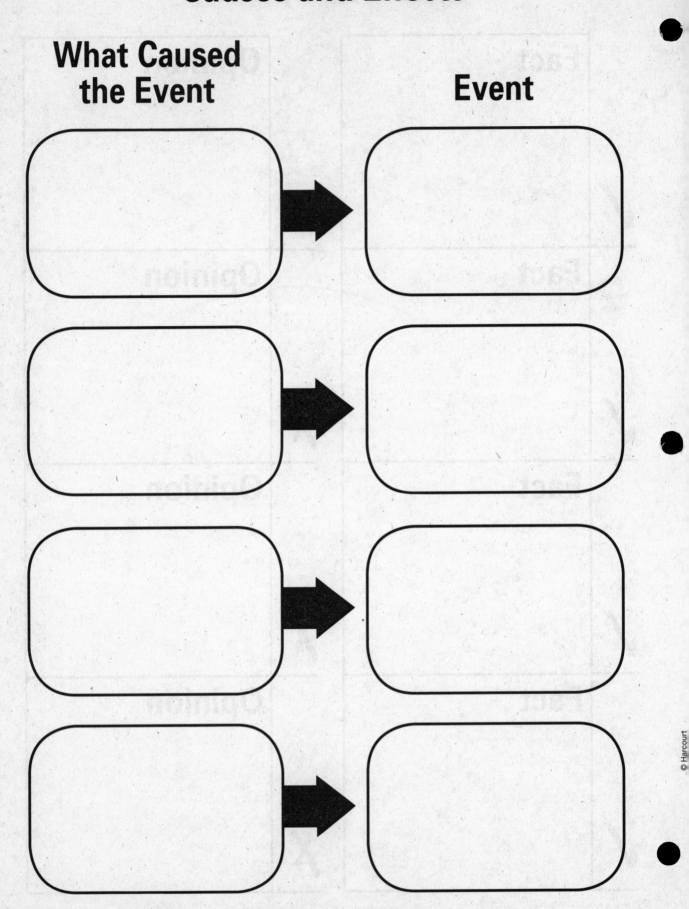

What Caused the Event

Event

© Harcourt

Compare and Contrast

Categorize

Sequence

Event
Order

Event

Event

Event

Event

Summarize

Important Facts

SUMMARY

Important Facts

Make a Generalization

Fact

Fact

GENERALIZATION

Fact

Fact

Draw a Conclusion

What You Already Know

What You Learned

CONCLUSION

Point of View

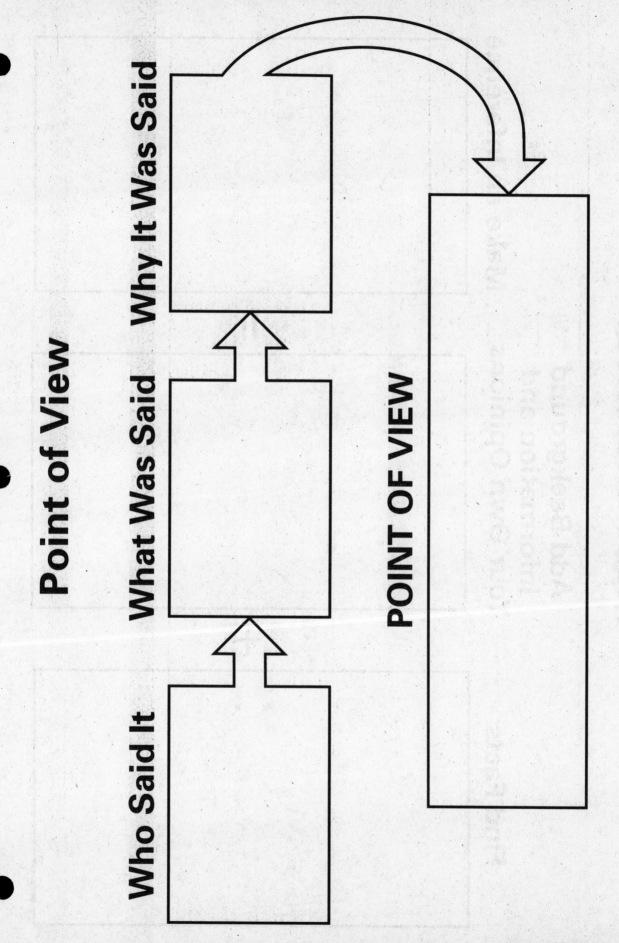

Who Said It

What Was Said

Why It Was Said

POINT OF VIEW

Make Inferences

Add Background Information and Your Own Opinions

Make an Inference

Find Facts

=

+

Generalize

The United States

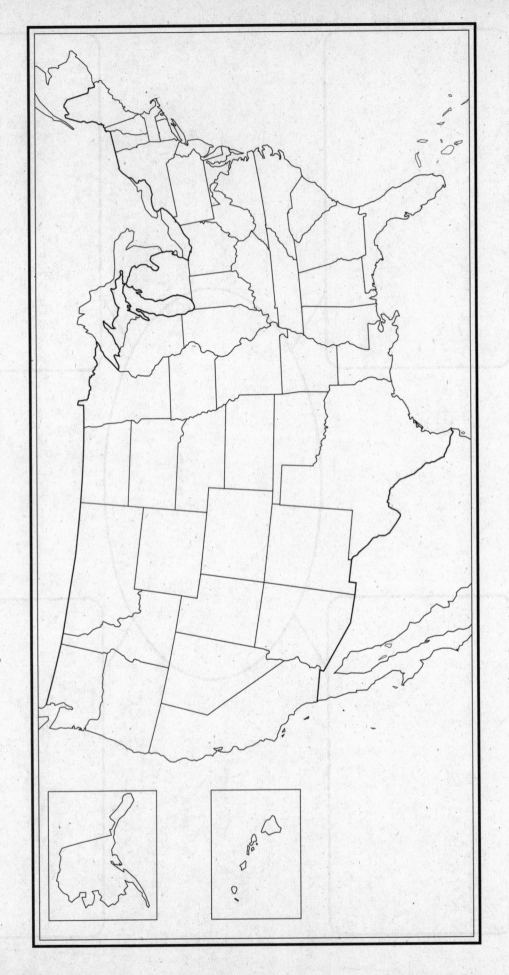

North America

The World

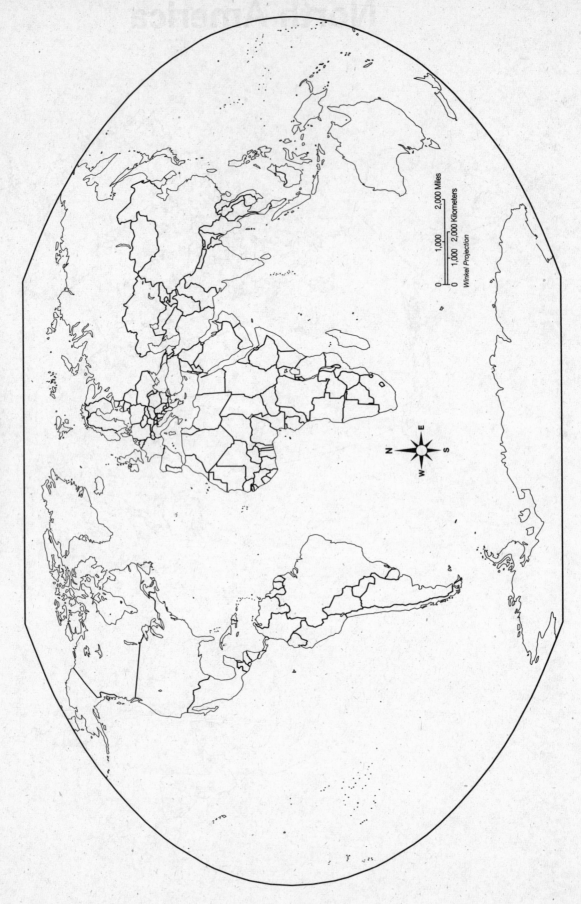

2,000 Miles

1,000

0

2,000 Kilometers

1,000

0

Winkel Projection

N E S W

Eastern Hemisphere

Western Hemisphere

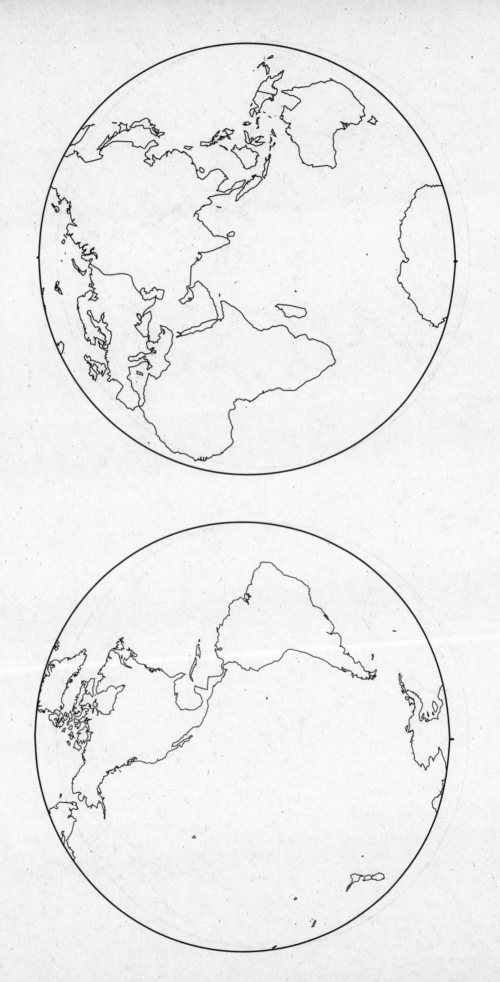

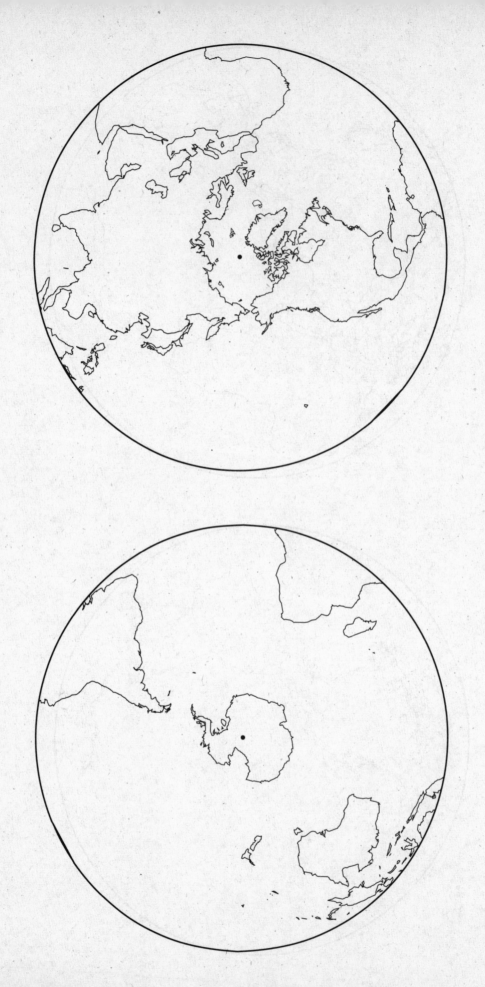

Northern Hemisphere

Southern Hemisphere

Planning Options

♦ individual   ♦♦ partners   ♦♦♦ group/class

	Activity	Materials	🕐	Link	
Drama Activity pages 6–9	**Good Morning!** Students read a readers theatre play about three families living in different communities.		30 min.	U. 1, Ch. 2, Les. 1–3	♦♦♦
Simulations and Games pages 10–11	**Town Meeting** Students simulate a town meeting and discuss how to use a new parcel of land.	paper, pencils	45 min.	U. 1, Ch. 1, Les. 1	♦♦♦
	Guess My Community Students play a guessing game in which they try to guess a group member's "secret location."		30 min.	U. 1, Ch. 1, Les. 1–3	♦♦♦
	Checker Directions Students move checkers to learn about directionality.	checkerboards, checkers, self-stick notes, spinners	30 min.	U. 1, Ch. 1, Les. 1	♦♦
	Mystery Map Students play "Battleship" using real maps or images as the background.	grid map, overhead projector (optional)	30 min.	U. 1, Ch. 2 Les. 1	♦♦♦
Long-Term Project pages 12–13	**Class Wall: Communities All Around Us**			U. 1, Ch. 2, Les. 1, 2, 3	♦♦♦
	Week 1 Introduce the project. Students brainstorm a list of words that describe their community.	posterboard, markers	30 min.		
	Week 2 Students investigate a particular community in order to make a diorama.	reference books and materials, Internet access	90 min.		
	Week 3 Students complete their dioramas and create a poster about the community they studied.	shoe boxes, paper, posterboard, pens, pencils, markers or colored pencils, craft sticks, glue, tape, other art materials as needed, reference materials, Internet access	90 min.		
	Week 4 Students present the exhibit.	posterboard, markers, camera (optional)	90 min.		

© Harcourt

	Activity	Materials	🕐	Link	
Short-Term Projects pages 14–15	**Map It!** Students create maps of their communities.	large construction paper, markers, pens, pencils, a map for reference	20 min.	U. 1, Ch. 1, Les. 4	👤
	Regional Sort Students create cards representing urban, suburban, and rural scenes.	old magazines, catalogs, travel brochures, scissors, index cards or construction paper pieces, glue or paste	45 min.	U. 1, Ch. 2, Les. 1, 2, 3	👥👤
	My Dream Community Students create mobiles that display the characteristics of their dream communities.	coat hanger, string, hole punch, paper or index cards, markers or crayons, old magazines, glue or paste, scissors	30 min.	U. 1, Ch. 1, Les. 4	👤
	Where Have We Been? Students list the states they have lived in or visited and discuss the data.	wall map of the U.S., pushpins, chart paper, markers	30 min.	U. 1, Ch. 1, Les. 1	👥👤
Writing Projects pages 16–17	**Faraway Friends** Students write a letter describing their community.	paper, pencils	30 min.	U. 1, Ch. 1, Les. 4	👤
	What Is a Community? Students write essays about their community.	paper, pencils	30 min.	U. 1, Ch. 1, Les. 1	👤
	Travel Pamphlet Students create a travel pamphlet.	travel pamphlets, paper, pencils	60 min.	U. 1, Ch. 1, Les. 3	👥👥
	Observation Journal Students respond to their surroundings.	paper, pencils	60 min.	U. 1, Ch. 1, Les. 4	👥👥
	Letter to the Editor Students write letters to the editor about a local issue.	paper, pencils	45 min.	U. 1, Ch. 1, Les. 4	👤
	Picturing Stories Students write stories in response to a picture.	photograph of a community, paper, pencils	30 min.	U. 1, Ch. 2, Les. 1, 2, 3	👤
Why Character Counts pages 20–21	**Caring** Students read about caring and complete a follow-up activity.	pencils	30 min.	U. 1, Ch. 1, Les. 3	👤
Economic Literacy pages 22–23	**Location and Choice** Students read about making decisions about where to live and complete a follow-up activity.	pencils	30 min.	U. 1, Ch. 2, Les. 1, 2, 3	👤
Citizenship Pages 24–25	Students read about freedom, hold a discussion, and complete a writing activity.	pencils	30 min.	U. 1, Ch. 2 Les. 1, 2, 3	👤

© Harcourt

♦ individual ♦♦ partners ♦♦♦ group/class

	Activity	Materials	🕐	Link	
Drama Activity Pages 28–31	**Wait! Don't Pollute!** Students read a readers theatre play about the importance of reducing pollution.		30 min.	U. 2, Ch. 4 Les. 3	♦♦♦
Simulations and Games pages 32–33	**Geography Concentration** Students match cards representing geography terms with corresponding definitions.	index cards	45 min.	U. 2, Ch. 3, Les. 2	♦♦♦
	A Solution to Pollution Students hold discussions to find solutions to the pollution problem.		30 min.	U. 2, Ch. 4, Les. 3	♦♦♦
	It's All Relative Students give relative location clues to help group members find a location.	map with states labeled, compass rose	20 min.	U. 2, Ch. 3, Les. 2	♦♦♦
	Draw That Physical Feature Students try to guess a physical feature based on a drawing.	chalkboard, writing utensils, timer, index cards	30 min.	U. 2, Ch. 3, Les. 2	♦♦♦
	How Would Life Change? Students discuss how life would change if they lived in a different region of the country.		45 min.	U. 2, Ch. 3, Les. 3	♦♦♦
Long-Term Project pages 34–35	**Class Presentation: Landforms Exhibit**			U. 2, Ch. 3, Les. 2	♦♦♦
	Week 1 Introduce the project. Students brainstorm a list of landforms.	posterboard, reference material, maps, atlases	30 min.		
	Week 2 Students investigate a particular landform in order to make a model.	reference materials, Internet access	90 min.		
	Week 3 Students complete their models and add additional written information.	reference materials, Internet access, paper, pencils, notecards	90 min.		
	Week 4 Students present the exhibit.	tables, camera (optional)	60 min.		

© Harcourt

	Activity	Materials	🕐	Link	
Short-Term Projects pages 36–37	**Chart of Regions** Students list characteristics of the five main U.S. regions in a chart.	reference materials, posterboard, markers	30 min.	U. 2, Ch. 3, Les. 3	
	Location Tower Students create location towers.	large construction paper, markers, crayons, pens or pencils	30 min.	U. 2, Ch. 3, Les. 1	
	Landform Maps Students construct landform maps of their communities.	large construction paper, markers, crayons, pens, pencils, glue, craft sticks	60 min.	U. 2, Ch. 3, Les. 2	
	Geography and Music Students learn songs celebrating geographic features or places.	tapes, records, or CDs featuring songs about geographic places or features; music books (optional); instruments (optional); sheets with lyrics (optional)	30 min.	U. 2, Ch. 3, Les. 2	
Writing Projects pages 38–39	**Landform Poems** Students write poems about landforms.	paper, pencils	30 min.	U. 2, Ch. 4, Les. 2	
	Write an Art Review Students review art work of landscapes or landforms.	paper, pencils	30 min.	U. 2, Ch. 3, Les. 2	
	Human Nature Students write a persuasive essay about the environment.	paper, pencils	30 min.	U. 2, Ch. 4, Les. 3	
	Reasons to Conserve Students write an essay about conservation.	paper, pencils	30 min.	U. 2, Ch. 4, Les. 3	
	Natural Disaster Guidebook Students write a guidebook that describes natural disasters and methods of preparing for them.	paper, pencils, reference materials	45 min.	U. 2, Ch. 4, Les. 1	
	Landform Legends Students write legends that explain the creation of a landform.	paper, pencils	30 min.	U. 2, Ch. 3, Les. 2	
Why Character Counts pages 42–43	**Respect** Students read about respect and complete a follow-up activity.	pencils	30 min.	U. 2, Ch. 4, Les. 3	
Economic Literacy pages 44–45	**Scarcity** Students read about scarcity and complete a follow-up activity.	pencils	30 min.	U. 2, Ch. 3, Les. 4	
Citizenship Pages 46–47	**National Parks** Students read about national parks, hold a discussion, and complete a writing activity.	pencils	30 min.	U. 2, Ch. 3, Les. 2	

UNIT 3 Planning Options

👤 individual 👤👤 partners 👤👤👤 group/class

	Activity	Materials	🕐	Link	
Drama Activity pages 50–53	**Paul Revere's Ride** Students read a readers theatre play about the start of the American Revolution.		30 min.	U. 3, Ch. 6, Les. 3	👤👤👤
Simulations and Games pages 54–55	**Match-Up** Students draw pictures of inventors/inventions and explorers/lands explored on index cards and use them to play games.	index cards, pencils, crayons or markers	30 min.	U. 3, Ch. 5, Les. 3	👤👤👤
	Town Meeting Students simulate a town meeting about town development.	resource materials, paper, pencils	45 min.	U. 3, Ch. 6, Les. 2	👤👤👤
	Morse Code Students use the Morse code alphabet.	Morse code alphabet, paper, pencils	20 min.	U. 3, Ch. 5 Les. 3	👤👤
	Made-Up Games Students come up with original games.		30 min.	U. 3,	👤👤👤
	American Time Line Students create a time line of American history.	rope or string, wood pinch-style clothespins, index cards, tape	30 min	U. 3	👤👤👤
Long-Term Project pages 56–57	**Class Presentation: Pioneer Day**			U. 3, Ch. 6, Les. 4	👤👤👤
	Week 1 Students study pioneers' lives.	books on pioneer life and living skills, photographs, models	40 min.		
	Week 2 Students collect information, materials, and supplies for the presentation.	reference materials, assorted materials as needed	60 min.		
	Week 3 Students finish their projects and prepare identification cards.	manila folders, markers	60 min.		
	Week 4 Students present their projects on Pioneer Day.	student-prepared materials, seating area, camera (optional)	60 min.		

© Harcourt

	Activity	Materials	🕐	Link	
Short-Term Projects pages 58–59	**Now That's Inventive!** Students identify a problem and create an invention to solve it.	posterboard, markers, crayons, pencils, index cards	45 min.	U. 3, Ch. 5, Les. 3	🧍
	Compass Navigation Students learn to use a compass.	simple magnetic compasses	30 min.	U. 3, Ch. 6, Les. 1	🧍🧍🧍
	Commemorative Stamps Students design a commemorative stamp.	index cards, drawing supplies, pinking shears (optional)	45 min.	U. 3, Ch. 5, Les. 2	🧍
	Language Chart Students complete a bar graph of languages spoken by members of their families.	tally table, grid paper	30 min.	U. 3, Ch. 6, Les. 1	🧍🧍🧍
Writing Projects pages 60–61	**Letter from an Explorer** Students imagine they are explorers discovering your community.	paper, pencils	30 min.	U. 3, Ch. 6, Les. 2	🧍
	Family Stories Students record a family anecdote.	paper, pencils	60 min.	U. 3, Ch. 6, Les. 1	🧍
	What I Admire Most Students write an essay explaining what they admire most about early Americans.	paper, pencils	45 min.	U. 3, Ch. 6, Les. 2	🧍
	What a Change! Students compare their communities in the past and present.	paper, pencils	30 min.	U. 3, Ch. 5, Les. 1	🧍
	Poetic Communities Students write a poem about an ancient community.	paper, pencils, reference materials	45 min.	U. 3, Ch. 5, Les. 4	🧍
	Biographical Sketch Students write a brief biography of a pioneer.	reference materials, paper, pencils	60 min.	U. 3, Ch. 6, Les. 4	🧍🧍🧍
Why Character Counts pages 64–65	**Fairness** Students read about fairness and complete a follow-up activity.	pencils	30 min.	U. 3, Ch. 6, Les. 1	🧍
Economic Literacy pages 66–67	**Technology** Students read about technology and complete a follow-up activity.	pencils	30 min.	U. 3, Ch. 6, Les. 3	🧍
Citizenship pages 68–69	**Equality** Students read about equality, hold a discussion, and complete a writing activity.	pencils	30 min.	U. 3, Ch. 6, Les. 2	🧍

UNIT 4 Planning Options

👤 individual   👥 partners   👥👤 group/class

	Activity	Materials	🕐	Link	
Drama Activity pages 72–75	**Listen to the Candidates** Students read a readers theatre play about a school election.		30 min.	U. 4, Ch. 7, Les. 1	👥👤
Simulations and Games pages 76–77	**Trial** Students simulate a trial.	resource materials	45 min.	U. 4, Ch. 7, Les. 2	👥👤
	States and Capitals Students play a game by identifying states and capitals.	large outline map of the U.S., small beanbags	30 min.	U. 4, Ch. 8, Les. 3	👥👤
	Word Jumble Students solve word jumbles about government and citizenship.	paper, pencils	30 min.	U. 4	👤
	Government Quiz Students play a quiz game based on government vocabulary words.	index cards	30 min.	U. 4	👥👤
Long-Term Project pages 78–79	**The Four Freedoms Mural**			U. 4, Ch. 7, Les. 1	👥👤
	Week 1 Introduce the project and students review "The Four Freedoms."	images of President Franklin D. Roosevelt, Norman Rockwell's paintings of "The Four Freedoms"	45 min.		
	Week 2 Students make sketches for their section of the mural.	butcher paper, assorted art supplies, old magazines, glue, scissors	60 min.		
	Week 3 Students complete the mural and prepare an introductory statement.	butcher paper, assorted art supplies, collected images, lined paper	60 min.		
	Week 4 Students present their mural.		30 min.		

© Harcourt

	Activity	Materials	🕐	Link	
Short-Term Projects pages 80–81	**Becoming a U.S. Citizen** Students ask a visitor why, when, and how he or she applied for U.S. citizenship.	index cards	45 min.	U. 4, Ch. 7, Les. 1	
	Rhymes of America Students recite poems about the United States.	*A Book of Americans* by Stephen Vincent Benet	30 min.	U. 4, Ch. 7, Les. 1	
	Safety Walkabout Students review rules and laws about safety.	clipboards, paper, pencils	60 min.	U. 4, Ch. 8, Les. 1	
	Ideas for Voting Students use an idea web to analyze the voting process.	chart paper	30 min.	U. 4, Ch. 7, Les. 2	
Writing Projects pages 82–83	**Hero Sketches** Students write a character sketch.	paper, pencils	30 min.	U. 4, Ch. 7, Les. 3	
	Campaign Speech Students write a campaign speech.	paper, pencils	45 min.	U. 4, Ch. 7, Les. 1	
	Election Posters Students create election posters.	Internet access, social studies reference books, drawing paper, pencils	45 min.	U. 4, Ch. 7, Les. 1	
	Research a State Bird Students write a report about your state bird.	reference material, paper, pencils	30 min.	U. 4, Ch. 8, Les. 4	
	Citizenship Poem Students write a poem about citizenship.	paper, pencils	30 min.	U. 4, Ch. 8, Les. 2	
	Classroom Bill of Rights Students create a Bill of Rights for the classroom.	paper, pencils	30 min.	U. 4, Ch. 7, Les. 1	
Why Character Counts pages 86–87	**Patriotism** Students read about patriotism and complete a follow-up activity.	pencils	40 min.	U. 4, Ch. 8, Les. 4	
Economic Literacy pages 88–89	**Public and Private** Students read about public service and private business and complete a follow-up activity.	pencils	30 min.	U. 4, Ch. 8, Les. 1	
Citizenship Pages 90–91	**Voting and Elections** Students read about the election process, hold a discussion, and complete a writing activity.	pencils	45 min.	U. 4, Ch. 7, Les. 1	

Planning Options

🧍 individual   🧍🧍 partners   🧍🧍🧍 group/class

	Activity	Materials	🕐	Link	
Drama Activity pages 94–97	**A New Life** Students read a readers theatre play about immigration.		30 min.	U. 5, Ch. 9, Les. 1	🧍🧍🧍
Simulations and Games pages 98–99	**New National Landmarks** Students hold a mock committee meeting.		45 min.	U. 5, Ch. 9, Les. 3	🧍🧍🧍
	Category Spin Students identify famous American sites and events.	5-part spinner, pencils, 5-column tally sheets	30 min.	U. 5, Ch. 9, Les. 3	🧍🧍
	What's That Term? Students give clues for important words and concepts from the unit.	index cards	40 min.	U. 5	🧍🧍🧍
	True or False? Students answer true or false questions about important events from the unit.	pair of cards labeled "T" and "F" for each group	30 min.	U. 5	🧍🧍🧍
	Coming to America Students role-play immigrants coming to America.		30 min.	U. 5, Ch. 9, Les. 1	🧍🧍🧍
Long-Term Project pages 100–101	**Multicultural Pageant**			U. 5	
	Week 1 Introduce the project and students discuss multiculturalism.		45 min.		🧍🧍🧍
	Week 2 Students create a flag representing their assigned culture.	large sheets of butcher paper, crayons, markers, paints, brushes, photographs, reference materials as needed	60 min.		🧍🧍
	Week 3 Students prepare further contributions to their project.	reference materials as needed	90 min.		🧍🧍🧍
	Week 4 Students present their projects for the pageant.	student-prepared materials, camera (optional)	45 min.		🧍🧍🧍

	Activity	Materials	🕐	Link	
Short-Term Projects pages 102–103	**Mapping Population** Students create a population density map.	reference materials, Internet access, enlarged outline map of your state, drawing supplies	45 min.	U. 5, Ch. 9, Les. 1	👥
	Landmarks Pamphlet Students create pamphlets about American monuments and landmarks.	reference materials, Internet access, crayons or markers, paper, pencils, large map of the U.S., yarn, pushpins	60 min.	U. 5, Ch. 9, Les. 3	👥
	Immigration Over the Years Students study the changes in U.S. immigration from 1900 to 2000.	reference materials, construction paper, ruler, markers	45 min.	U. 5, Ch. 9, Les. 1	👥
	Happy Holidays! Students create posters that represent a holiday celebrated in another culture.	reference materials, large construction or drawing paper, art supplies, index cards	30 min.	U. 5, Ch. 9, Les. 3	👤
Writing Projects pages 104–105	**Flag Folding Directions** Students write directions for folding a flag.	flags, towels, scarves, or fabric; paper, pencils	30 min.	U. 5, Ch. 9, Les. 3	👥
	Praising Diversity Students write an essay explaining what multiculturalism means to them.	paper, pencils	30 min.	U. 5, Ch. 10, Les. 1–3	👤
	Lady Liberty Literature Students respond to a book about the Statue of Liberty.	books about the Statue of Liberty, paper, pencils	45 min.	U. 5, Ch. 9, Les. 3	👤
	Fables Students write a fable that teaches a lesson.	paper, pencils	60 min.	U. 5, Ch. 10, Les. 1	👤
	What's Your Custom? Students write about a family custom or tradition.	paper, pencils	45 min.	U. 5	👤
	Class Cookbook Students create a class cookbook.	reference materials, Internet access, paper, pencils	30 min.	U. 5, Ch. 10, Les. 1–3	👥👤
Why Character Counts pages 108–109	**Responsibility** Students read about responsibility and complete a follow-up activity.	pencils	30 min.	U. 5 Ch. 10, Les. 1	👤
Economic Literacy pages 110–111	**Competition** Students read about competition and complete a follow-up activity.	pencils	30 min.	U. 5, Ch. 9, Les. 2	👤
Citizenship Pages 112–113	**Life, Liberty, and the Pursuit of Happiness** Students read about life, liberty, and the pursuit of happiness, hold a discussion, and complete a writing activity.	pencils	30 min.	U. 5, Ch. 9, Les. 1	👤

Planning Options

🚶 individual 🚶🚶 partners 🚶🚶🚶 group/class

	Activity	Materials	🕐	Link	
Drama Activity pages 116-119	**All Business** Students read a readers theatre play about a child-owned business.		30 min.	U. 6, Ch. 11, Les. 1–3	🚶🚶🚶
Simulations and Games pages 120–121	**Mail-Order Shopping** Students pretend to order goods to furnish a cabin using a catalog.	all-purpose catalogs from general retailers, calculators, pencils, paper	45 min.	U. 6, Ch. 11, Les. 4	🚶🚶🚶
	Product Possibilities Students play a game about natural resources.	paper, pencils, timer	20 min.	U. 6, Ch. 11, Les. 2	🚶🚶🚶
	Barter Day Students barter with objects brought from home.	various items	30 min.	U. 6, Ch. 12, Les. 1	🚶🚶
	Trade Treasure Hunt Students learn about where goods originate.	index cards, world map, pushpins	30 min.	U. 6, Ch. 11, Les. 3	🚶🚶🚶
Long-Term Project pages 122–123	**Community Marketplace**			U. 6	🚶🚶🚶
	Week 1 Students brainstorm ideas about business.	advertisements, reference materials, chart paper, markers	45 min.		
	Week 2 Students create business plans.	paper, Internet access	60 min.		
	Week 3 Students complete their advertisements and pamphlets for their booths.	drawing paper, art supplies, Internet access	60 min.		
	Week 4 Students present their business ideas to the class.	student-prepared materials, display area	90 min.		

© Harcourt

	Activity	Materials	🕐	Link	
Short-Term Projects pages 124–125	**Market Research** Students study features and origins of goods in grocery stores.	clipboards, pencils, paper	60 min.	U. 6, Ch. 11, Les. 3	
	Budget Your Allowance Students create a budget.	paper, pencils	30 min.	U. 6, Ch. 12, Les. 3	
	High-Tech Mural Students create a mural about new technology items.	butcher paper, catalogs and magazines, glue, markers	45 min.	U. 6, Ch. 11, Les. 4	
	Survey of First Jobs Students interview an adult about his or her work experience.	paper, pencils	45 min.	U. 6, Ch. 12, Les. 3	
Writing Projects pages 126–127	**Job Wanted** Students write and respond to a job advertisement.	paper, pencils	30 min.	U. 6, Ch. 12, Les. 3	
	A Biography Students write a biography of a businessperson.	reference materials, Internet access, paper, pencils	60 min.	U. 6, Ch. 11, Les. 1	
	Kid Power Students respond to *Newsies*.	a copy of the film *Newsies*, paper, pencils	45 min. plus time to view movie	U. 6, Ch. 12, Les. 2	
	Business Resources Students write a report about a business in the community.	reference materials, Internet access, paper, pencils	60 min.	U. 6, Ch. 11, Les. 1–3	
	What If . . . Students write a story about a world without technology.	paper, pencils	30 min.	U. 6, Ch. 11, Les. 4	
	Commercials Students create a commercial.	paper, pencils	45 min.	U. 6, Ch. 11, Les. 4	
Why Character Counts pages 130–131	**Trustworthiness** Students read about trustworthiness and complete a follow-up activity.	pencils	40 min.	U. 6, Ch. 12, Les. 2	
Economic Literacy pages 132–133	**The Internet** Students read about the Internet and complete follow-up activity.	pencils	30 min.	U. 6, Ch. 11, Les. 4	
Citizenship Pages 134–135	**Jobs** Students read about jobs, hold a discussion, and complete a writing activity.	pencils	45 min.	U. 6, Ch. 12, Les. 2	

Answer Key

Unit 1

Daily Geography (pp. 18–19)
1. Washington D.C.
2. a way of life of a group of people
3. the weather that a place has over a long period of time
4. desert
5. one of the shapes that make up the Earth's surface
6. Atlantic Ocean and Pacific Ocean
7. plain
8. ocean
9. an area of land with its own people and laws
10. communities located in different nations that become partners to learn more about each other
11. a huge ocean wave
12. a community's location
13. compass rose
14. north, south, east, west
15. northeast, northwest, southeast, southwest
16. an area with at least one feature that makes it different from other areas
17. the number of people living in a place
18. city
19. car
20. Patapsco
21. a protected place with deep water that allows ships to come close to shore
22. the movement of people and goods
23. south
24. Virginia, South Carolina, Tennessee, and Georgia
25. the exact location of a place
26. a small city or town built near a larger city
27. suburban
28. the countryside, away from cities and large towns
29. Arkansas
30. the raising of farm animals and the growing of crops for sale

Why Character Counts (p. 20)
Answers will vary but should include an example of helping someone in need.

Character Activity (p. 21)
1. Answers will vary. Possible answers: hospitals, community centers, libraries, churches
2. Answers will vary. Possible answers: medical care, education, food
3. Answers will vary. Possible answers: help younger child tie shoelaces, help around the house, be friendly to a new student

Economic Literacy—Try It (p. 23)
Answers will vary but should show an understanding of the differences between the city and country.

Citizenship (p. 24)
1. Answers will vary but should demonstrate an understanding of the definition of freedom.
2. Answers will vary. Possible answers: freedom to choose where one lives, freedom to say what one feels, freedom to dress as one pleases

Write About It (p. 25)
Answers will vary but should display an understanding of the importance of freedom.

Unit 2

Daily Geography (pp. 40–41)
1. a model of Earth
2. North America, South America, Europe, Asia, Antarctica, Australia, Africa
3. North America
4. hemisphere
5. equator
6. a line that shows where a state or country ends
7. the position of a place in relation to other places
8. the borders of cities, states, and countries
9. the exact position of a place
10. plains or Great Plains
11. range or chain
12. Appalachian Mountains
13. valley
14. a landform with steep sides that rise to a flat top
15. a plain
16. the Great Lakes
17. the Mississippi River
18. the gradual wearing away of Earth's surface
19. the plants, animals, land, water, and climate that make up an area
20. a place's main physical features
21. West, Southwest, Midwest, Southeast, Northeast
22. renewable
23. the physical features and human features of a place
24. highway
25. tornado
26. to speed up travel between the Atlantic and Pacific Oceans
27. irrigation

28. a huge structure built to hold back water
29. anything that makes a natural resource dirty or unsafe to use
30. the protecting of natural resources to make them last longer

Why Character Counts (p. 42)
Answers will vary. Sample answer: It means to take care of Earth by not polluting or littering.

Character Activity (p. 43)
Answers will vary. Sample answers:
1. trees, water, fuel, air
2. conserve natural resources
3. pollution, littering
4. clean up trash, use less water

Economic Literacy—Try It (p. 45)
1. Answers will vary. Sample answer: I could start by giving each person only one juice box. That way I know the juice will last me for a long time.
2. Answers will vary. Sample answer: Natural Resource: Trees; Ways to Conserve: plant more trees for each one cut down, use a source other than wood to heat homes

Citizenship (p. 46)
Answers will vary.

Write About It (p. 47)
Answers will vary but should display an understanding of the uses of park lands. Sample answers: Reasons to save park lands include recreation, conservation of natural resources, and quality of life. Reasons to use park lands include natural resources that heat homes and fuel cars, and water power.

Unit 3
Daily Geography (pp. 62–63)
1. Illinois
2. Many people passed through and some chose to stay; it was easier to get goods and services to places built along transportation lines.
3. horseback, ship, foot, wagons
4. train
5. telegraph
6. a large group of people living in a well-organized way
7. Asia
8. Africa
9. Greece
10. the Tiber River
11. all the land and people under the control of one nation
12. salt and cloth
13. a traveling group of traders
14. desert

15. a place for ships to dock and drop off or pick up goods or people
16. a person who goes first to find out about a place
17. west
18. a new community
19. Little Rock
20. Mexico
21. France
22. the Mississippi River
23. settler or immigrant
24. Massachusetts
25. colony
26. East Coast
27. west
28. the Rocky Mountains
29. Alaska and Hawaii
30. 50

Why Character Counts (p. 64)
Answer will vary. Sample answer: The colonists thought that British rule was unfair because they did not have any say in the laws created for the colonies. As a result, the colonists declared war on Britain. They hoped that winning the war would give the right to make their own laws.

Character Activity (p. 65)
1. Answers will vary. Possible answer: It is not a good idea for one country to make the laws for another country because people should be allowed to make their own rules and laws.
2. Answers will vary. Possible answer: We can bring fairness by making sure it doesn't happen again.

Economic Literacy—Try It (p. 67)
1. Answers will vary. Sample answers: the Internet, telephones, mp-3 players, computer games, cell phones
2. Answers will vary. Possible answer: Technology allows me to do things much faster. When I want to research a topic, I can use the Internet. I can find information on the Internet much faster than I can by looking in the library.
3. Answers will vary. Possible answer: Sometimes when new things are invented, experts do not know the long-term effects of them. For example, doctors do not always know how new medicines will affect people in the future.

Citizenship (p. 68)

1. Answers will vary.
2. Possible responses: Over time, the idea that "all men are created equal" has changed. Long ago, the Declaration of Independence only applied to certain groups. African Americans and Native Americans, as well as many others, were not treated equally. Now all American citizens are treated equally.

Write About It (p. 69)

Answers will vary. Possible answer: Martin Luther King, Jr., helped make sure all Americans enjoy the same rights before the law. Today, all children can go to public schools together.

Unit 4

Daily Geography (pp. 84–85)

1. Indianapolis
2. Alabama
3. Annapolis
4. Washington, D.C.
5. a part of a state that has several towns or cities within its borders
6. county seat
7. Denver
8. INDIANApolis and OKLAHOMA City
9. North Dakota and South Dakota
10. Montpelier, Vermont
11. Idaho
12. south
13. Raleigh, North Carolina; Columbia, South Carolina
14. Honolulu
15. Answers will vary.
16. Alaska and Hawaii
17. south or southeast
18. Kansas
19. Tennessee
20. Indiana
21. New Mexico
22. Maryland and Virginia
23. the state capital
24. Philadelphia, Pennsylvania
25. Washington, D.C.
26. Baltimore, Maryland
27. Mexico
28. Canada
29. Asia
30. the Himalayas

Why Character Counts (p. 86)

Answer will vary. Possible answer: You can show patriotism by flying an American flag and by saying the pledge.

Character Activity (p. 87)

1. Answers will vary. Possible answer: You say the pledge at the beginning of a school day, perhaps in school assemblies. Saying the pledge means that you are patriotic and loyal to your country.
2. Answers will vary. Possible answer: You sing it before baseball games. It is about the perseverance of our country.
3. Responses will vary, but students should write a poem that expresses their pride in the nation.

Economic Literacy—Try It (p. 89)

1. public and private
2. public
3. public and private
4. public and private
5. public
6. public and private
7. public and private
8. public
9. public and private
10. public and private
11. public and private
12. public and private
13. private
14. public
15. private
16. public and private
17. public and private
18. private
19. public and private
20. public and private

Citizenship (p. 90)

1. 18; Answers will vary.
2. You should care because he or she will help shape the world you live in.

Write About It (p. 91)

1. Students should name the current President.
2. Students should name the current Vice President.
3. Students should name the party the current President and Vice President belong to.
4. Students should name the senators from your state.
5. Students should name the governor of your state.
6. Students should name the representative from your area.
7. Answers will vary.
8. Answers will vary. Possible answer: Leaders shape a community by working to create new laws and by deciding how public money should be spent.

© Harcourt

Unit 5

Daily Geography (pp. 106–107)
1. The steep mountains made traveling there difficult; people there did not visit other communities.
2. someone who comes from one country to live in another country
3. the western coast; Angel Island
4. the Atlantic Ocean
5. north
6. west; northwest
7. Ellis Island
8. San Francisco Bay
9. Mexico
10. to move within one's own country
11. Northeast, Midwest, and West
12. The region has a mild climate.
13. the number of people living in an area of a certain size
14. city
15. Answers will vary.
16. a group of people who share the same language, culture, and way of life
17. Lake Erie
18. an important natural or human feature that marks a location
19. France
20. New York
21. South Dakota
22. Nigeria
23. Guatemala
24. Ireland
25. Mexico
26. Spain
27. 50
28. 40
29. South
30. Brazil

Why Character Counts (p. 108)
Answers will vary. Possible answer: People have a responsibility to help their community because their community helps them.

Character Activity (p. 109)
1. Answers will vary. Possible answers: house chores, following the rules, treating others with kindness
2. Answers will vary. Possible answer: following the rules
3. Answers will vary. Possible answers: taking care of ourselves, making sure we eat good food

Economic Literacy—Try It (p. 111)
1. Answers will vary: Possible answers: create new advertisements, lower prices, make a better product
2. Answers will vary. Possible answer: Business B will probably shut down. Business A's lower prices are taking customers away from Business B. Over time, Business B will not have enough customers to keep the store open.

Citizenship (p. 112)
1. the rights to life, liberty, and the pursuit of happiness
2. Immigrants hoped that the United States would give them opportunities. They wanted to have better jobs and education. Many immigrants thought that the beliefs of the United States would help them reach their dreams.

Write About It (p. 113)
Answers will vary.

Unit 6

Daily Geography (pp. 128–129)
1. Illinois
2. a natural resource that can be used to make a product
3. workers who produce goods and services
4. how the land in a certain area is used; where products are grown or made in an area
5. explanations for the symbols used on the map
6. Answers will vary.
7. The cold climate does not allow them to grow fruit.
8. a large, flat boat
9. the buying and selling of goods between countries
10. a good brought into one country from another country
11. a good shipped from one country to another
12. steel; corn; electronics; wheat, and/or cars
13. China and Indonesia
14. Japan
15. China
16. newsprint paper
17. Louisiana, Alabama, and Mississippi
18. business that is done electronically, for example, on the Internet
19. a form of trade without the use of money
20. Europe, the European Union
21. India and Thailand
22. Turkey
23. Philadelphia, Pennsylvania
24. Washington, D.C., or Fort Worth, Texas
25. an economy in which people can make and sell any product or service allowed by law
26. New York City
27. Scarcity means that the supply of a product is not enough to meet the demand for it.

28. Tokyo
29. Africa
30. Atlantic Ocean and Indian Ocean

Why Character Counts (p. 130)
Answers will vary. Possible answer: People show trustworthiness when they follow the rules and tell the truth.

Character Activity (p. 131)
1. Answers will vary. Possible answers: Show up on time; follow the rules and procedures of the workplace; treat fellow workers, bosses, and customers with respect; do your job thoroughly and on time; do not steal or lie; respect other people's property and privacy
2. Answers will vary. Possible answers: Pay you in full and on time; see that working conditions are safe, clean, and fair; treat you with respect; help you when you need it
3. Answers will vary. Possible answers: Pay you in full and on time; treat you with respect; do what they say they are going to do and when they promise; follow through on tasks

Economic Literacy—Try It (p. 133)
1. Responses will vary. Be aware that some students may not have online access in their homes.
2. Responses will vary.
3. Answers will vary. Possible answer: The Internet has made it easy to bank, shop, and communicate with others. Now I do most of my banking online and keep in touch with people through e-mail.
4. Possible responses: unwanted intrusions, advertising, or sales calls; loss of freedom; loss of confidentiality; worries about private matters becoming public.
5. Anytime you give a company personal information, you need to be careful.

Citizenship (p. 134)
1. the Constitution
2. Constitution Day is a holiday that is celebrated on September 17. People use this day to remember why the Constitution is important.

Write About It (p. 135)
Answers will vary, but should contain an explanation of why the student is interested in a certain job and how he or she might improve his or her chance of getting the job through education and training.